Timothy Green Beckley's

THE
AUTHENTIC
BOOK OF
ULTRA-TERRESTRIAL
CONTACTS

GLOBAL COMMUNICATIONS

TIMOTHY GREEN BECKLEY'S
THE AUTHENTIC BOOK OF ULTRA-TERRESTRIAL CONTACTS

By Timothy Green Beckley

Cover Graphics by Tim R. Swartz

INTERIOR ART BY LORENZO SOUTHERLAND

This book is dedicated to my good
friend and a fellow truth seeker
Charla from Tucson.

Global Communications
P.O. Box 753
New Brunswick, NJ 08903

mrufo8@hotmail.com

www.conspiracyjournal.com

Don't Miss Out On Free Audio CD Offer - Page 174!

CONTENTS

Native Venusian as drawn by Dr. Wanda M. Lockwood

ENCOUNTERING THOSE CRAZY ULTRA-TERRESTRIALS

FOR nearly 50 years, I have been amassing incredible UFO reports and stories of close encounters with "aliens" who I prefer to identify as Ultra-Terrestrials because none of us can be certain of their true origins. Yes, some could be legitimate ETs, but we have no definite way of proving this theory, so its each to their own when it comes to verification.

Regardless of their home stomping ground, we can't deny they have been cunning, cagey and crafty. We can't believe for one minute what they tell us, because they seem to change their modus operande and personal narrative with every single close encounter. In addition, who can accept as gospel the word of any being that can shape shift in front of our eyes? From an alien to a gnome in less than sixty seconds does not built up confidence.

In the course of my UFOlogical career I have seen and heard just about everything. I am never amazed anymore at the bizarre claims that I have to deal with. They come to me either directly from those involved, or from what I consider to be credible sources. As editor of such publications as *UFO Review*, and *UFO Universe* there has been such a continuous stream of raw data that I now possess over 50 file drawers crammed with all sorts of data of varying quality.

Today there is a multitude of postings on the internet pertaining to UFOs, but as far as I am concerned there is no way of checking on the validity of these incidents. In the "old days" we relied a lot on the mass media - both local and international - for information. And usually as much effort as possible was put into authenticating the story before it was printed. You at least knew the individuals mentioned in the clippings on hand were not a figment of the imagination of some editor over at the *Weekly World News*, a weekly tabloid that regularly lampooned the subject even if some gullible readers didn't realize they were being put on. The book you are now about to delve into contains some of the best reports and encounters that fascinate me the most. They are as spine tingling to me now as they were when they originally appeared in print. They were clipped out of newspapers most of us have never heard of and sent to me by a legion of associates worldwide. Very few other researchers possessed the network of freelance stringers that I did.

Though it's gotten more difficult to verify some stories because of the unanimity of the world wide web, I do my best to maintain a certain standard before I will say I absolutely believe in something.

Last year, I received a call from a Toronto-based production company. CINEFLIX is the outfit behind "William Shatner's Weird Or What?," a paranormal "fact or fiction" show that is in its third season, airing on the History Channel Canada. Currently, you can't "officially" view this program in the States, but it's immensely popular north of the U.S. border. Now I should stipulate that I first met Shatner back stage at Dick Clark's *$10,000 Pyramid* game show sometime in the 1970s.

William Alan Shatner is a Canadian actor, musician, recording artist, author and film director whom just about everyone adores. He has a charming sense of humor and a down to earth charismatic personality. Over the years, Bill and I have shared a mutual friend and I even spent an hour in jail due to a misunderstanding of the hilarious kind. The unprovoked incident took place while Shatner was performing with a philharmonic orchestra inside in the world famous Madison Square Garden arena. The circumstances that surround this story are too complex to go into right now and are not relevant to the matter at hand anyway. But it still causes a chuckle or two whenever I relate the circumstances around this "misdemeanor" - at the time - not so uproarious episode.

I can say this much for sure - Bill loves a challenge. He is not above doing almost anything to cause a stir and to draw attention to his performance art, even if it might seem a bit hokey or silly to some. "Captain Kirk" is as fascinating in real life as he obviously was to millions of adoring fans who remember him from the Star Trek days of his career. He always has been hard pressed to say NO! to any opportunity presented to him, even if it requires him to recite poetry or to record a selection of his favorite songs, including "Rocket Man" and "Bohemian Rhapsody."

In order to set the stage for my recent invitation to appear on "William Shatner's Weird Or What?" I have to turn back the clock to our initial meeting. I was working at the time as a freelancer for several of the national tabloids including *the Enquirer*, *the Star* and the somewhat seamier scandal sheet known as *Midnight*.

This was in the days before having to stalk a celebrity to get a good story was required by such publications. I met dozens of well-known personalities and on a more or less equal basis. Some of them wanted to hear all about UFOs and the paranormal as much as I wanted to hear about their careers.

Did a UFO Save the Life of Brother Bill?

Canadian born actor and Star Trek stalwart William Shatner wanted to tell me about his own UFO experience, and so we arranged to meet back stage at the Ed Sullivan Theater in NYC, where he was taping a week's worth of the *$10,000 Dollar Pyramid* hosted by Dick Clark.

"I'll tell you a story that happened to me, and is open to any kind of interpretation you wish," Shatner began. The story he told me was to become his often quoted epic encounter with a spaceship that he felt at the time had nothing to do with his having been a character in a weekly televised science fiction series.

"In the late '60s, when Star Trek was on, there were a lot of UFOs being sighted in the desert near Palmdale, California. We heard all kinds of stories about these objects, crafts, spaceships - call them what you will. There was even one fellow who said he talked with creatures from space. During this period, I used to drive my motorcycle a great deal, and would occasionally head for the wide-open span of sand and sun. With my sense of humor, I'd say to myself, 'Well, if I were a little green man in a flying saucer and wanted to get publicity' - which is what they would seem to be seeking -who would I contact faster than Captain Kirk of the Star Ship Enterprise?'" Shatner says he would often wonder if they were capable of picking up the thoughts of earthlings.

"One day I was out driving with four other guys, around noon - that's the hottest part of the day in the desert - when I hit a hole and fell from my bike. I must have fainted when the bike collapsed on top of me. When I came to, I estimate that I was unconscious for only about a minute, I couldn't get my motorcycle started. The motor refused to turn over. . . So here I am in the middle of the desert with a metal helmet on, wearing a leather jacket, heavy pants, boots and a machine next to me worth close to five thousand dollars."

Shatner didn't want to leave the bike behind but it was definitely too heavy to carry or even push along. It was at this point that he happened to see something gleaming in the blistering sunlight.

"It was like when you have a nightmare and you feel something crawling over your body or wrestling with you. As you awaken from the dream it turns out your blanket was the thing crawling over you. In other words, it was more of a sensing - a feeling - a shadowy phantom. All I know, positively, is that I suddenly felt better. As I said, when I came to I couldn't get the bike to move. No matter what I did it refused to start.

"Finally, I tried pushing it up a hill, but it wouldn't go in that direction. Then I turned around and decided to go down the hill, but it still wouldn't budge. Nor did it obey my command to turn left. Eventually, I shoved it to the right and it began to move as though it was going some place on its own. But this time I was doing what I was feeling. One could say I was doing what I was told to, but I was just doing the easiest possible thing.

"Fantastic as it may seem, the motorcycle appeared to have a way of going on its own. At this point I thought I saw somebody – another cyclist – in the distance waving me on, and so I continued to struggle with the heavy metal monster until I stumbled upon civilization in the form of a gas station in the middle of the desert, resting at the side of an old paved road."

A production still from "William Shatner's Weird or What?" TV series shows him to be a world-class ghostbuster. Wonder if that device is any good for detecting a Djinn?

Shatner seems to be saying that this "other cyclist" was some sort of sinister phantom – possibly a Man-In-Black. Because when this figure joined the pack of Shatner's biking buddies they would have assumed it was Bill trailing behind, when in actuality he was wandering about stranded and possibly ready to die in the desert heat. Though I apparently was Shatner's prime target to relate this experience to, because he knew it was going to appear before the Enquirer's almost three million readers in those days, as far as I know he repeated this extraordinary tale numerous times to other interested parties.

Some critics may say that Shatner created this account for the sake of publicity. I got chastised numerous times for my accepting his story at face value. I was always quick to point out that I was not on assignment to seek testimony from a pilot or a police officer, nor was it necessary to conduct a polygraph examination. This was more or less an entertainment piece, not a scientific inquiry, and so I let it go at that. Did his potentially life saving UFO experience really happen, or can we put it down as an urban legend of the Mojave Desert told by one of the most entertaining actors of our time?

Recently, in the last few months, Shatner revealed during a TV interview that he had concocted the entire incident, I would surmise to get some non-Star Trek media attention, as all celebrities must garner some form of publicity if they are to stay at the top of their game.

I have been asked if I am offended that Shatner "took advantage" of the situation and used me in effect as a patsy to grab the limelight and possibly boost his "ratings" among UFO fans who are not usually all that thrilled by Star Trek and science fiction in general?

Not at all! It was a wonderful story and it paid my overdue electric bill at the time, I am sure. Like I say, there was no call for a close scrutiny of the events Bill Shatner related. But it seemed to be a well thought out story; still, Bill is an actor and that's what good actors do best - create believable stories that will live on (like Shakespeare?).

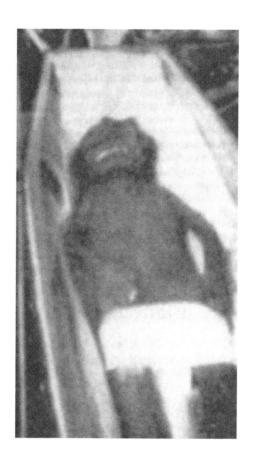

I was shown this supposed mummified alien by the late Ralph Lael, who claimed that it was part of a group of Ultra-Terrestrials inhabiting the interior of Brown Mountain, where mysterious lights and fireballs have been reported for hundreds of years.

Dead Micro Mini "Alien" Caught in Trap By Mexican Farmer
"Weird or What?" William Shatner Wants to Know

But now let's speed up and time travel ahead to the present day. Somehow CINEFLIX got wind of what they thought would be a great story to dramatize as part of Shatner's series for the Canadian counterpart of the History Channel. The Canadian cable outlet airs some of the same shows that the History Channel in the U.S. does, but they also have original programming of their own which CINEFLIX produces a great deal of, and very adequately, I might add. I spent three days in Toronto as we went over every minute detail of what we were going to film. If it were Major Donald Keyhoe he might have flipped out (like he did on the Armstrong Circle Theater because, though the show was not "scripted," we did have certain perimeters to work within.

It was my old friend Joshua P. Warren, host of "Speaking of Strange" - broadcast every Saturday night out of Ashville, NC - who originally hooked me up with the Toronto production company who was looking for "someone in authority" to confirm the legitimacy of a tiny creature caught by a Mexican farmer in a large animal trap that had been dubbed "an alien space baby" by the easily excited press in that country.

I remembered that Josh had talked about this "remarkable" finding on the Dark 30 Hour portion his show and had posted a picture of the alien baby on his website www.SpeakingOfStrange.com. Warren is a real character, a true showman, and so it's hard to define "real" in his world. Josh is a filmmaker, like myself, and we share a lot in common, including a pint of brew from time to time. We met at a horror film fest and didn't realize that each of us was an expert in the paranormal. Josh is a certified ghost hunter supreme and probably the world's leading expert on the mysterious Brown Mountain Lights seen in dense forest and mountains around Morgantown.

Hundreds have gotten up close and personal with these lights and Joshua has even videotaped one (and this is for real!). One of the old timers living on the mountain, a fellow named Ralph Lael, had claimed to have journeyed inside the mountains, met with aliens at an underground base there and even had one of the visitors laid out in a coffin under the counter at his long crumbled Outer Space Museum at the very point where the forestry department has set up a roadside stop so tourists can attempt a sighting of the lights themselves. After buying one of his booklets that told his "entire story," he would bring out the little creature which resembled a pigmy more than it did an alien. I had snapped a shot or two of the creature in the coffin and it had been published and posted with the proclamation that I had proclaimed it an actual alien corpse. **NOT TRUE!**

But, hey, a good story is a good story and so I let it ride. Nevertheless, when Shatner's people contacted me about verifying the alien baby caught in a trap in Mexico I told them outright that I was skeptical. Even I don't want to ruin my credibility. After studying stills of the creature and a video or two I told the CINEFLIX staff that there is no way I could go on "William Shatner's Weird or What" and declare this a true extraterrestrial.

However, upon closer examination, I wasn't ready to write the little tike off completely. Minus its skin layer, the sinister looking carcass did appear strange and unusual - I know Shatner would prefer the word "Weird" in there somewhere and I was willing to go that far.

The legend goes that the farmer Marao Lopez had captured the creature, shown it to a few of his farm hands and when it squawked and lunged for them (what would you do if you were tangled up in a nasty trap?) they did the only thing that came to mind . . . they dipped the creature into a vat of acid which pealed off his skin and killed him.

The men eventually took their possession to a university in Mexico and they were told that it was like nothing born of this earth, though it did have some components that appeared human (like a hybrid?) The scientists said the creature could not have been a mutant of any time as it had no DNA and all living things should have DNA. Tests revealed a creature that is unknown to scientists - its skeleton has characteristics of a lizard, its teeth do not have any roots like humans and it can stay underwater for a long time (well, if it's dead, that last statement has no meaning).

Though one wants to be sorry for the "alien baby" captured by a Mexican farmer, one should save one's sorrow, as the farmer was burned to death in a horrific fire after putting this creature on display.

Supposedly, we hear on good authority that the farmer who caught the creature in the trap (there was said to be a second one who escaped) died shortly after all this attention when he was in a bad car accident and burned to a crisp. A case of the Ultra-Terrestrials seeking revenge?

My notion was, and this was what I told Shatner's producers, that the creature could not have been a space being. First off, it was too tiny and fragile to wheel itself about at the speed of light. And where was the craft that it arrived on Earth in? And what about the lack of breathing apparatus? And how could a super smart alien (it had an enlarged brain, the examining scientists had said) get himself caught in such a primitive trap? It didn't add up, as far as I was concerned, to something extraterrestrial, that's for damn sure.

But what of another possible explanation?

In the book "*Round Trip To Hell In A Flying Saucer*," we dealt with the existence of the Djinn, a shadowy race of demonic creatures known in the Islamic faith as living in another dimension and for the most part cursing humans and committing dastardly deeds. They often appear as smoke and possess people just like the devil would do in our Western culture. And the thing is, if you compared a picture or illustration of the Djinn, they offer up a reasonable resemblance to the alien baby of Mexico. And so exactly what is a Djinn(often spelled Jinn)?

Well, we know about the Genie in the bottle from "A Thousand and One Arabian Nights," but otherwise most of us who are not of the Islamic religion don't really know the story/nature of the Djinn and who they really are. Easily put into the category of Ultra-Terrestrials, they are not the nicest of entities.

The following is a definition that seems most prevalent . . .

The word "Djinn" translates as anything that is concealed or invisible. The Djinn are a race that have no defined physical form of their own, so they are therefore invisible to the naked eye. However, they are shape shifters who can take on the physical form of just about anything they want. Many say that they walk among us every day.

With his flesh still attached, this little Djinn, supposedly photographed hanging off the side of a cave wall, looks suspiciously similar to the alien baby sans skin captured in a metal trap in Mexico.

This is a head shot of the alien baby.

Weird or What? Not only would William Shatner like to know for his TV series, but so would independent researchers worldwide. Notice the resemblance to the head of a Djinn!

You will often see smoke when your Djinn appears, not because the smoke IS the Djinn, but because it accompanies him/her. It is simply a sign that your Djinn is nearby and ready to communicate, and signifies the presence of energy.

Djinn can also appear with orbs, streaks of light, mists or other kinds of phenomena. It can be a big, awe-inspiring appearance, or a subtle, almost-not-noticed kind of appearance. With Djinn, like people, no two are exactly alike and there are countless ways they may manifest.

Some Djinn will never manifest in any kind of physical form, but that doesn't mean that they aren't there and watching you. These Djinn will generally communicate with you only during dreams or meditation. They aren't any more or less powerful than other Djinn, they just choose to present themselves differently.

So I took a shot and took the train to Toronto where I lauded my theory of the Djinn. I am sure this is the first time the subject of aliens versus the Djinn has been discussed on a widely viewed television program. Of course, my statements were broken up into brief sound bites but I do believe I got the message across to Shatner, as well as his very obliging producers and crew, that all strange looking beings do not have to come from a place far, far away in another galaxy, but might be hear living right alongside us. We could almost reach out and touch them . . . and possibly some of us have.

The world of Ultra-Terrestrials is a mystifying one, and there is a lot to learn about those that seem flesh and blood one moment but can metamorphose, can alter their shape, size and appearance as well as their density.

Many of the cases which I have detailed in this work take up the subject in a serious manner. There are many strange things in the pages within that are about to unfold.

There is actually a dual purpose to this book. First off, we have endeavored to show that close encounters with UFOnauts or alien space beings are not as rare as some people might imagine. In fact, the files of the world's only flying saucer newspaper — *UFO REVIEW* — contain somewhere between 1500 and 2000 cases in which face-to-face confrontations between earthlings and the occupants of flying saucers have taken place. We are not talking about a series of isolated events, but a worldwide phenomenon that involves every nation upon which our sun shines. South America, Africa, the Middle East, Russia, China... you name the place, and in all likelihood, contact with UFOs has been established.

Your first question might be, "Why haven't I read about these contacts in my local newspaper?" Well, the truth is that for the most part, the news media has remained surprisingly silent about a subject that is bound to effect each and every man, woman and child now residing on this planet. It might be that they remain uninformed when it comes to UFOs (and have no place to turn to for accurate information), or it could be - as some maintain - that they are part of an "organized plan" to keep the truth a closely guarded secret AT ALL COST. This, I would think, is probably not true in the case of many small town dailies and weeklies which continue to print saucer sightings and related incidents from time to time, but might reflect a gem of reality when it comes to such a prestigious publication as the New York Times, who, after all, is more concerned about "international events" rather then interplanetary ones.

This is not to say that anyone can verify one hundred percent, every single case we have reviewed in this book. More then anything else, I have tried to give a general "overview" of the situation as a means of pointing out that there are many strange and unknown aspects to this mystery we are desperately trying to crack. There are various ways to approach this enigma. From the material we have gathered, it is obvious that many, many races of beings from "somewhere out there" are making themselves right at home on Terra Firma regardless of whether we approve or not.

It is also apparent from the cases we have looked into, that our friendly "Space Brothers" are interested in speaking with us. They want to communicate as they have a definite message to get across, however, the majority refuse to listen. Perhaps because their method of communication is NOT normally with the spoken word. Their language is frequently symbolic. Often, they try to tell us things in a form of visual images through their deeds and tasks while on the earth. Those who have "second sight" can hear them telepathically or can make contact through meditation. Upon occasion, they will even beam a message over radio or television into an individual's home (or into the homes of an entire community).

This book, offers various methods for attempting contact with alien beings who wish to communicate with those who are open-minded enough to listen. We are told that "motive and desire" are uppermost in our "getting through" to them. These highly advanced beings are said to be both intellectually and spiritually advanced. They converse with you only if you are "worthy" and follow their instructions for extraterrestrial contact to the letter.

To some whose consciousness may be limited, much of what has been recorded in this book will seem "far fetched." and they may consider these ideas and theories to border on the edge of lunacy or, at best, impossibility. But, if all of us harbored such feelings we might still be living in the Dark Ages without a car, telephone, television, and other appliances that make our life much easier. One TV manufacturer now has a set you can answer your telephone through. Perhaps someday it will be a matter of turning a particular dial and speaking with our alien friends who dwell out among the stars.

We invite you to participate in one of the most important experiments of all time - contact with extraterrestrial and ultra-terrestrial beings. Let us know your results.

Timothy Green Beckley
NYC June 2012
mrufo8@hotmail.com

Can you ever believe I was that young? Here I am at Jim Moseley's National UFO Conference held in 1967 in NYC looking goo goo eyed at Orthon, The man from Venus.

CHAPTER ONE: THEY ROAM THE EARTH

To say we are not alone in the universe is to over simplify the truth. According to the testimony of any number of individuals it would appear that aliens arrived on Earth awhile back, and because so many of them look remarkably human, they have managed to infiltrate our society quite easily. Naturally, every strange person you come in contact with is not of extraterrestrial origin, but a small percentage of them may be. That is if we are to believe the following stories, told by what seem to be hones individuals.

* * *

Sinda Angulo De Montiel writes a regular column for Panorama, a newspaper published in Maracaibo, Venezuela. Though we don't know what her past involvement - if any - with UFOs might have been, it's apparent that she now considers the subject of prime importance.

"STRANGER" GIVES DIRE WARNING

"I thought about it a long time before deciding to do this article. Generally subjects of this nature are taken with joking and indifference, but an uncontrollable impulse, accompanied by a Venezuelan and Christian-like necessity, obliges me to make public what I will now transcribe. I should point out that this anecdote, which took place in Caracas three weeks ago, was related to my sister-in-law and me by two personal friends, a couple worthy of all confidence, one of them being the director of a department in a well-known company in the state of Zulia (western Venezuela; capital is Maracaibo).

"The case is as follows:

"Two co-eds in psychology at the Catholic University (one of them a close relative of the above-mentioned couple) were in a coffee house in Sabana Grande one evening late last month, when they were approached by an individual with all the apparent characteristics of an ordinary citizen. Upon asking him what he wanted, he answered them that he was an extraterrestrial being and that his mission was to warn that Caracas was going to be partially destroyed by a very strong earthquake on August 28 of the present year. The two students considered it a joke, and tried to ignore him. The man with dark glasses (he had sun glasses on) defied them by listing what they had in their wallets without them having to be opened. He described it in detail; nevertheless, they just called him a "sort of magician." Therefore* the extraterrestrial asked one of them to put her hand under the palm of his hand, which he had extended in the air, and suggested that she try to take it away; though wanting to do it, the youth could not: her hand was paralyze' To make sure that the girls did not doubt the truthfulness of the event, the mysterious personage asked them to look carefully at him, he took off the dark glasses, and showed them a face without eyes, like with closed eyelids. In the face of this clear demonstration the girls became receptive, and controlling their nerves they could converse a little with the extraterrestrial. He communicated to them that they did not have five senses as we do, but seven which let them perceive such phenomena before they begin. He told them that the places most affected by the earthquake would be Los Faios Grandes, La Florida, La Castellana, and adjacent areas (like Sabana Grande, they are all eastern suburbs of Caracas - trans.), but that all of Caracas would suffer irreparable damage. He told one of the students - the one who had put her hand under his palm - that she would not live to see the disaster, as she'd suffer an incurable illness which would lead to her death ;he declared that this was impossible, that she was completely healthy and hat she did not feel anything special.

"After saying the necessary (good-bye) the man walked away out of light. Days later, as a coincidence or perhaps to further stress the demonstration, a first cousin of one of these two girls, who was already informed about what happened in Sabana Grande, was passing by the small plaza in front of the Central University and found a girl friend with a very bad fit of nerves, who told her that she had just spoken with a personage with the same characteristics as the one who appeared to the two previous girls, except that this time the extraterrestrial told her that the earthquake would occur between August 28 and September 28 of this year.

"Here ends the account. I don't know what to tell you; I feel the same as you people, between half-surprised and frightened. In particular, I believe in the existence of other living beings. Why should we think that we are the only ones with the right to live in such a big universe? If this (the prediction) does not happen it would be ideal, and it would be just one more article. But if it does happen? I hope that those who can, will take the necessary precautions to not be in Caracas during that time... The rest is up to the readers.

"Last Minute: I learned by a phone call from the man who related the above to us that in Caracas they put in the hospital the girl who the extraterrestrial had said would not live; she has galloping cancer, and no hope of surviving."

There are a number of cases to draw upon which give substance to our theory that aliens have cleverly made themselves at home next door to us. These are three cases taken from my own personal files which would seem to add support to a seemingly far-fetched idea.

THEY LOOK LIKE US!

During the summer of 1966, a Gallipolis, Ohio, nurse saw a dome-shaped UFO land in a remote field outside of town. She was compelled to leave her auto and walk toward the craft. Several seconds passed before a number of beings emerged from the UFO and walked up to the woman, who found herself unable to move from nervousness and fear. The woman said the aliens looked exactly like earthlings and spoke to her for several minutes in perfect English.

Eventually, the ship departed and the woman rushed into town to report her experience. She went immediately to the sheriff's office and told aim what had happened. The law enforcement official laughed at her and told tier to go bother someone else.

Months later, while walking along the street, she saw these same two men. Again, she ran into the sheriff's office in an attempt to drag him out to see the "space people" for himself. Once again he refused. Since then she has been constantly ridiculed by her neighbors and now refuses to discuss the case with anyone, though she continues to maintain that these UFOnauts are living in her community. (Credit for story: John A. Keel)

While lecturing at a small college in the Midwest, researcher James W. Moseley, was told an incredible story by a professor in his mid-fifties who approached him after his speech.

The professor told the former editor-publisher of *Saucer News* that a local resident, whom he had known for upwards of twenty-five years, was driving toward town one afternoon when she suddenly saw a strange ship resting on tripod legs. As she approached the craft, she observed a normal looking woman and two men standing near the vehicle. They were talking to each other and eventually walked over to a parked auto and drove off. The witness apparently tried to stop the car, a Ford, to see what was going on. However, her attempt was in vain, because the men and woman swerved around her, nearly causing her to drive into a ditch.

The weirdest part of this encounter is yet to be told! The college professor continued by telling investigator Moseley that the woman wasn't overly frightened by what she had seen. Since the saucer occupants were so human in appearance - not some sort of monsters- this tended to put her fears at ease.

In fact, over a period of weeks, she began to relax, her life returning to normal, and she eventually even managed to push her unworldly encounter to one side of her mind. Then suddenly she was thrown back into the void of the irrational once again! This time it happened not out in the country, but downtown in the local supermarket. The woman was shopping for the weekly groceries when she noticed, over at the next counter, a familiar-looking face. Edging closer, she was shocked to find that it was the same "person" who was seen months before, driving off from a UFO, leaving her at the side of the road.

The bewildered woman followed the UFOnaut, the female of the trio, to the check-out counter. Once they were both in line the witness said, "Haven't I seen you somewhere before?" With this, the "space woman" bolted from the line, leaving her parcels next to the cash register and disappeared out onto the street - never to be seen again.

A New York City woman, Barbara Hudson, had repeated UFO sightings as a child living in the Harlem Section of Manhattan. One day after leaving school, she was driven by several ordinary looking men to a rural area of Pennsylvania. In a secluded field surrounded by a forest she saw other men and women walking around outside of an object which stood on tripod landing gear. The men who had driven her to this locale said that they would make contact with her from time to time and would disclose things that would benefit her. They warned her about speaking of her experiences, as they said, "nobody would listen." Ms. Hudson maintains that the operators of this craft are known as "The Group," and that they have several bases here on earth. One is in New England, where Barbara has traveled on several occasions to meet with other aliens whom she says mingle freely in our society, taking jobs and going about their business undetected.

In a recent issue of GRAY BARKER'S NEWSLETTER, Gray Barker published a short, but curious letter from West Coast subscriber, Emma Martinelli, concerning the alien known as Orthon which contactee George Adamski claimed to have met many times. Emma reconfirmed her story in a personal letter to me and I find her little tale most interesting since it tends to prove that at least some of the aliens we are dealing with are quite human.

"In reviewing my UFO library, going back to 1952 and there on, I'm amazed to find so few writers who believed in George Adamski. I'm not saying he was perfect. Who is? I speak from experience for I knew Adamski personally for 17 years.

"One instance: One day in San Francisco a very presentable young man came to my door. He said Mr. Adamski had sent him to me.

"The story? This young man, whom I will call Bill, had been sitting in the Greyhound Bus Depot. He was at the end of the line... an alcoholic. He had only the bus fare over the East Bay Bridge to Oakland. God knows — maybe he was going to take a leap from the bridge. Well, along comes a wonderful looking man and takes Bill in hand. He took Bill to the Hotel Ogden (now closed). This beautiful stranger put Bill to bed. And in passing, Bill said that this stranger was just as human as my earth-man. Bill watched this stranger shower and should know.

"Next morning the stranger took Bill to breakfast. I don't recall .n exact detail, but I think the stranger stayed with Bill in the little hotel the preceding night, maybe to watch over our earth guy. Bill said i very strange thing happened at breakfast: A man at the other end of the counter came to the stranger and said, in rather harsh tones, "Goddammit! You stop reading my mind!" And with that he left. I am presuming from what Jill told me that after this hotel experience, Bill was put back on the right path again. But the following is the part that stays with me...

"Bill felt he should go south and see Adamski. Naturally, everyone knew Adamski, at least by his writings. Well, the first thing Bill saw on entering Adamski's foyer, was this painting of the stranger who had helped him in San Francisco! Naturally, the subject of this portrait was dressed in what we call a 'jump suit'. Long, golden hair and no mistaking the face. Bill was told that this man was Orthon, the man Adamski had met in the desert. Most really intelligent people are familiar with Adamski's account of this. Personally, I believe. I blushed to admit, however, that after 33 years in UFO work, only now am I pretty much convinced that we do have what I term "Star Guests" walking among us. Naturally, when one has lad "stranger" experiences on their own, maybe believing isn't so difficult, after all! We ourselves, are going out that-a-way in the physical, what's so amazing about more advanced civilizations beating us to the punch."

IDENTIFYING THE ALIENS AMONGST US

It has often been said that if you wish to make contact with those alien beings who are stationed on or around earth it is beneficial that you be able to call them by name so that they know of your peaceful intentions. The following Space People are among those most frequently mentioned by name in UFO and contactee literature.

ASHTAR — Commander in Chief of the Free Federation of Planets. Stationed on board a giant mother ship hovering near Saturn. Has been seen many times in visions and in physical form while on earth. Is said to have a beautiful violet aura and often dresses in flowing robes. Is in charge of a million space beings and is interested in spiritual development of mankind.

ORTHON — First made famous in George Adamski's book "*Flying Saucers Have Landed*," Orthon is a rather typical alien. Hailing from Venus, this spaceman looks typically human. He stands slightly under six feet tall, has blonde shoulder-length hair, and converses via mental telepath.

MONKA — A soldier for the cause of peace, Monka is a very favorite Martian entity who has channeled through many contactees. He is always outspoken on interplanetary affairs and has a wisdom that is light years beyond the most intelligent person on our planet.

AURA RHANES — A resident of the planet Clarion, Aura is captain of a "Scow", or flying saucer. She is approximately 4 ft., 6 in. tall, is dark complexioned, looks as youthful as any young college girl and has dark hair and often wears a beret with a pleated skirt and black velvet blouse.

It is said that if you call them by name they may appear to you.

CHAPTER TWO: INSIDE THE SAUCERS

FOR some, their stories are difficult to believe. After all it's one thing to claim to have seen a UFO and another to say you've had the privilege to go for a ride in one.

During the early 1950's such accounts were fairly common, but mostly they were brushed aside by both the public as well as the UFOlogical Community. Yet such far-fetched stories persist FROM ALL OVER THE WORLD to this day. My files must contain somewhere around 500 cases of this nature, and I'm probably only hearing a small percentage of them.

Before political tension started to build in Iran, that nation was experiencing a large number of UFO encounters, no doubt as a symbolic warning of the troubles that would soon plague this country. Perhaps Gholam Reza Bazargani could add some light on his experiences if we could locate him today. His little adventure caused a considerable stir in the Iranian Press after his "voyage" took place. The following is from an English language clipping dated April 7, 1976.

FROM CHALUS TO ISFAHAN BY UFO

It all began when 19-year-old Gholam Reza Bazargani, belonging to a wealthy and respectable family of Chalus, decided to take a stroll in the nearby woods on Sizdehbedar day.

It ended two days later in Isfahan, leaving in its trail a score of baffled policemen, puzzled psychiatrists, an unidentified flying object (UFO) and a lot of mystery.

According to Bazargani's report to Isfahan police, he was whisked away by a UFO on Sizdehbedar day while strolling through the forests, and landed in far away Isfahan on Sunday morning.

While the authorities immediately placed Bazargani under psychiatric examination to determine his sanity, other reports from villagers in Marvine and Lanjan near Isfahan poured in as if to confirm the young man's claims.

According to police officials in Isfahan, a number of people from these villages reported seeing what they described as a "flying saucer." Similar reports were also received from other individuals and groups from the same region. The time of observations in all these reports coincided with Bazargani's claims.

In Chalus, meanwhile, the police had launched a massive search for Bazargani, but there was no trace whatsoever of the young man. According to Bazargani, while he was walking alone deep in the forests on Friday he suddenly saw a UFO emerge from the sky, fly straight towards him and stop directly above him. He said he was unable to move as he watched four "beings" come out of the spaceship and take him inside it.

He claims that he spent some time under the scrutiny of the "beings" before passing out. "The next thing I remember is that I woke up back on earth early in the morning, not in the lush Caspian forests, but surrounded by barren lands," he said.

He somehow found his way to Isfahan later the same day. After spending a day with the police and psychologists, he traveled back to Chalus.

Although most authorities are skeptical about the whole affair, they are still mystified by so many identical reports coming from varied people.

All the doctors, including those at the Red Lion and Sun Society hospital in Isfahan, who examined Bazargani have given a clear report as to his health, both physical and mental.

For the next several months, UFOs were in the sky all over Iran. Jet fighters from the Imperial Air Force were even chased on several occasions by brightly lit objects, and thousands of Iranians spotted the discs while outdoors. On September 25, 1976, the Tehran Journal published the following story.

"I WAS TAKEN INSIDE THE FLYING SAUCER", MAN CLAIMS

The Ettela'at offices continued to be flooded with reports from people who claim to have seen flying saucers.

After last week's report of a UFO being chased by jets of the Imperial Iranian Air Force, newspaper offices were swamped by people claiming to have seen a "bright thing in the sky".

One man claimed yesterday that he had actually been kidnapped by strange beings, and taken inside a flying saucer. Ahmad Bani Ahmad, 56, a researcher in Iranian history, said he had been reluctant to tell the story of his encounter with beings from another planet earlier because he thought people would make fun of him.

Now, after so many people saw the UFO, he no longer fears ridicule. He said that last weekend, he and his wife were visiting Tabriz Lake. "My attention was caught by a glittering body that landed about 100 yards from my car. My wife and I were terrified. The round object was about four or five meters across, and there was a small window in the side. Two beings similar in shape to Egyptian mummies stepped out."

* * *

Such stories seldom receive wide spread attention. In most instances papers absolutely refuse to take such tales seriously and usually disregard them. That the UPI picked up an incident from South America and gave it coverage is a miracle in itself.

An Argentine trucker suffering from unexplained shock claimed during treatment with truth drugs he was taken aboard a flying saucer by aliens from another galaxy, it was reported today.

The newspaper *La Nacion* said a team of six doctors in Bahio Blanca, 400 miles southwest of Buenos Aires, have been treating trucker Dionisio Yanca since last October.

The daily newspaper said Yanca was first referred to doctors when he began suffering from a nervous shock that he could not explain. Under hypnosis and the truth drug, sodium pentothal, he said he had been taken aboard a space ship by aliens for an hour and a half, La Nacion said.

An unidentified flying object (UFO) was sighted by an Argentine air base near Bahia Blanca on the same day Yanca claimed he was abducted. Yanca said the space ship connected a hose to high tension wires and another to a small lagoon, apparently to take on electric power.

The newspaper said a local electric company reported a sharp and unexplained rise in power consumption at the time.

Dr. Eduardo Mata was quoted as saying he administered a truth serum to Yanca and "under the effects of sodium pentothal the patient said he spent an hour and a half aboard a UFO, but he cannot remember this when he is conscious."

Yanca reportedly said the aliens, whose humming voices were made intelligible by a loudspeaker, predicted the Earth would suffer grave events in the future.

He said they told him they had been trying since 1960 to determine whether man could survive in their galaxy if the Earth were destroyed.

In America, such "space flights" and brief visits aboard UFOs are happening all the time. As in the celebrated case of Betty and Barney Hill the witness may not have a clear recollection of what happened. We never did hear any more from Judy Kendell after this clipping from the Enterprise (Davis, Calif.) passed through our hands.

WOMAN IN TRANCE TELLS OF SPACE ORDEAL

Judy Kendell was kidnapped by space beings Saturday when a hypnotist put her in a trance to help her remember what happened to four missing hours of her life. The way the 23-year-old legal secretary told it, as she sat shivering on her warm living room couch in her Woodland apartment, the "old blue Ford" she was driving her two sisters home from Bodega Bay to Zamora in, was plucked up off the road somewhere on Interstate 505 near the Cache Creek Bridge.

They had left their grandmother's Bodega Bay home at 5:30 p.m. on a Sunday in November 1971 or 1972. It was normally only a three-hour drive but they didn't get home until midnight with no explanation for why the trip took so long.

All they remember was driving across the same bridge twice on a road with little traffic on a pitch-black night. Judy was realizing for the first time Saturday that she was kidnapped by a space ship.

A roomful of calm UFO researchers and incredulous friends watched Judy shield her face with her hands to prevent seeing a space creature she described as having a bulbous head with saucer-sized red pupiled gelatinous eyes.

She said it had no ears, "just holes."

The lower part of its almost translucent "milky" white face was covered with a mask she said while still clutching her face. But still she saw its neck which had red veins, "not like the purple ones we have."

She said its body was human looking and that it had five fingers on its hands, "like ours."

"But the head is so scary looking," she said. "It's coming toward me; I don't want to see it anymore. It's touching me!"

Judy said it touched her on the forehead and said in English that wasn't loud but sounded like it was muffled and coming through a distant megaphone, "it's okay, it's okay."

"But it's not okay," she said in a small tight voice. Suddenly she grabbed her right side and leaned over as if in pain. The hypnotist, Dr. W. C. McCall, who had flown up from Anaheim for this occasion, asked Judy what was happening.

"I feel like I got poked," she said.

McCall took her through the experience repeatedly. She got relaxed after being poked and was lying on a cold table with a sheet over her.

"They are taking urine out of me. They are catheterizing me," she said with expression of disgust passing over her face. "Uhhh."

She saw three different type creatures all dressed in grey standing at the foot of the table. She had no clear description of their faces. Strangely, she saw a regular human woman with straight black hair and blue eyes, who handed the creature a tube of colorless fluid, "that you can't see through."

The woman knew her name and was trying to reassure her. "I don't know how she knows my name," Judy said. "I don't remember saying anything to her."

For the most part, "nobody was saying anything," she said.

She got a pain at the top of her right thigh and held her hand on it, but she couldn't say what was happening.

"They are looking in my ear. I feel a strange thing there. It feels cold and hard inside," she said.

She said they were looking at her feet.

Throughout the ordeal, Judy kept complaining of a headache and clutching her head which at times she said felt like it was being "pressed tightly."

The creature placed a heavy metal machine over her eyes she said and she heard a quiet motor whirring inside. "Is it a brain reading machine?" McCall asked. "I don't know," she said.

When her head could move slightly, Judy saw what she described as a "round room" with windows all around. She saw two bucket seats at one side of the room with a "console with a lever like a car gear shift in the middle.

"There were three lights over the seats," she said.

She pointed to her left and said she saw a table with what looked like doctors' "probes" on it. She saw a black box there too with "speaker holes in it."

She said she couldn't see behind her where she said the machine that was put over her eyes came from. But she heard her sister, who wishes to remain unidentified and who won't have anything to do with this hypnotism, crying. "I can hear her calling my name. She is crying. She is really upset. She sounds far away. I hope she is alright," Judy said anxiously.

The next thing she said was that she was behind the wheel without really knowing how she got there.

McCall ran her through the experience again and she remembered the three grey clothed creatures carrying her by her hands and feet and throwing her into the car.

"They must have carried me because I couldn't walk," she said. She didn't know where her sisters were. They suddenly seemed to materialize, she said. When they were back in the car, it was pitch blank. And then...

"We just landed on the road - in my car!?" she said in a disbelieving voice. "In my car," she said with certain amazement.

They arrived in Zamora at about 12 midnight after crossing the Cache Creek Bridge on Interstate 505 twice. They had left Bodega Bay for the three-hour drive at 5:30 p.m. on a date they still can't pinpoint for certain.

The seven-hour drive remains almost as much a mystery as it was when they had no idea what happened.

Alvin Lawson, a professor of English at California State University at Long Beach and a UFO researcher, said Judy's story could be as much an idiosyncrasy in human makeup as an abduction by space creatures.

None of the researchers who in many ways were as mysterious as the story itself would say for certain how they felt about Judy's story.

McCall said he has hypnotized about six people with similar abduction stories. One of the problems is to get collaborating stories from both her sisters. But neither of them wants anything to do with reliving the experience. "They are scared to find out what may have happened to them," Judy said.

* * *

The case of Harry Joe Turner is truly a bizarre one. It must certainly rank among the most unorthodox of encounters, but it is a good example of what can happen to those individuals who undergo such a rare experience. I feel that I need not give this case any more of an introduction as this account by Bill McKelway in the September 23, 1979 issue of the Richmond, VA. Times-Dispatch says it all.

TRUCKER SAYS JOURNEY COVERED LIGHT-YEARS

He took a deep breath, inhaling another menthol cigarette and shifting his unwieldy 254-pound frame in a recliner where he muses in dreamy sleeplessness upon the events of the past harrowing weeks.

"Tell it in your own words, Harry Joe," said Harry Joe Turner's mother-in-law, Majorie Haymaker.

So Harry Joe Turner - truck driver, ex-Navy sharpshooter, amateur boxer, winner of 24 fights, loser of four, and donator of 27 pints of blood in his 28 years - exhales a plume of smoke and told it in his own words.

What unfolded over the next three hours was the incredible saga of how Harry Joe Turner and his 80,000 pound tractor-trailer rig, loaded with ketchup and mustard, were taken captive August 28 by alien beings, hauled off to an unidentified galactic community 6.8 light-years from Earth, and returned to a Fredericksburg warehouse a few hours later.

Since then Turner has been unable to work, he has sought psychiatric and neurological help in an effort to understand what happened to him; he has only partial use of his left side, and, most frightening, he said, he has been revisited by the aliens on at least two occasions.

"Ever since it all began," he said, "I've just been sitting here going over and over it in my mind trying to piece things back together. I'd feel pretty good if I could just figure out where I've been.

"If somebody would just come up to me and say I was drunk or something, that would be great because it would give me an explanation, a reason. But I wasn't drunk. Nothing makes sense."

He pounded another cigarette into the ashtray. "That's one of the reasons I'm willing to talk about all this. Maybe there's somebody out there who has had something like this happen to them. I need someone to help explain all this to me," Turner said.

He said that since the space odyssey, which allegedly took him 2.5 light-years beyond Alpha Centauri, his nerves have been shot, he has to rely on sedatives, he seems to be gaining "bionic strength" in his right arm, and he has "a craving" for such things as bananas, coconut and deer meat, items he never liked before.

"I never used to read anything but the Winchester Evening Star and Hustler magazine," Turner said. But now he goes through a variety of magazines, periodicals and religious literature with lightning speed, looking for clues to his ordeal.

"The only trouble is that I have to do a lot of the reading twice,

once for them and once for me. They're using my left eye to learn about the planet, I think," he said.

It all seems so ridiculous, so incredible, Turner said, but there are aspects of the incident that are soberingly convincing.

"It was a rainy night," Turner recalled, when he wheeled his 1974 Kenworth tractor and trailer out of The Bigman's Restaurant parking lot in Winchester, August 28.

He stopped a block away at a gasoline station and put 35 cents into a drink machine. He sipped his favorite soft drink, Mountain Dew, and glanced at his watch. It was 10:52. He was bound for Fredericksburg on a trip he'd never made before. "There was a little lightning and stuff, but the strangest thing was there was hardly no cars on the road. Everything seemed just deserted," he said.

Seventeen miles into the 80-mile trip, Turner had just crossed Paris Mountain and was heading south on U.S. 17 when he saw the lights of an approaching truck in the distance. "Hey, southbound 18-wheeler, where you going to, Buddy?" The driver of the other truck called over the citizens band radio. "And from that moment on," Turner said, pulling out another cigarette, "it was like I walked through that door right there into another world."

The lights of the truck kept blinking on and off. The CB screeched irritatingly and Turner cupped one hand over his ear while he kept his other hand on the wheel.

Then a brilliant light - "like from a helluva light bulb" - caught Turner's eye in the rear view mirror. He turned off his radio, but the grating sound grew worse and he cupped both hands over his ears.

A beam of almost palpably thick white light settled over the truck. Turner said, and the steering wheel no longer seemed to control the vehicle.

"It was like the whole truck was just floating like it was being vacuumed up into this thing. Now I still don't know what to call these things, but one of them opened the door and there was another one on the roof," Turner said.

He felt a tremendous pain in his shoulder, although he couldn't see a figure. "The thing had a grip like steel," he said. He grabbed a .32 caliber revolver, pushed the pistol to his left until he felt resistance and then fired eight hollow-point slugs.

"I went blam, blam, blam, blam, ... eight times, but the gun just seemed to move right through the thing. Nothing happened and then I started to just fade out. I shouted, 'My God, I can't kill the thing. What the. . .' and that was it".

The next memory, Turner said, was waking up in the warehouse parking lot in Fredericksburg. He has no idea how he got there. He was sitting on the passenger side of the truck and the seat belt on the driver's side was fastened.

His watch read 11:17, but a clock at the warehouse said it was 3 a.m. . Most curious was that two mileage indicators on the truck showed the vehicle had traveled only 17 miles since leaving Winchester, Turner said.

"After I got unloaded, I headed back to Winchester as fast as I could. There wasn't anything that was going to stop me," Turner said. The truck consumed 114 gallons of fuel, enough to make the 160 miles round trip more than three times.

Since the events of August 28, Turner said details of his otherworldly voyage have come back to him, details that he at first seemed unaware.

THE AUTHENTIC BOOK OF ULTRA-TERRESTRIAL CONTACTS

Speaking of his captors, he said, "My best recollection is that they were like you or me, only dressed in white clothes like a surgeon. They also had white caps and when they lifted up the fronts of them there were numbers, like identification numbers, written across their foreheads."

He struggled to recall landmarks and after hours of thought, the words "Alpha Centauri" came into his mind, a star 4.3 light-years from Earth he had never heard of before. He felt he had been taken to a city-like place 2.5 light-years beyond the star and there was a stop on the moon where he viewed astronaut Neil Armstrong's footprints.

Turner said the city apparently had undergone a nuclear holocaust long ago and it was the mission of the aliens to prevent such an occurrence on Earth.

"They want to help us, but they say things have gone pretty far here and that the end is coming soon," Turner said.

The aliens spoke in a language that he believes is called, or sounds like, Alpho Lazooloo. It sounds like a tape recording being played backward. To communicate with him, the aliens slowed their speech pattern, Turner said.

As he tried to put his life back together, Turner was visited by a band of six of the aliens, he said. They were invisible, but he said he was able to knock five of them to the ground.

On one occasion, Turner left the house only to return soaking wet for no apparent reason. He has crying spells, animals sometimes react strangely around him, and another time he went running from the house chased by the aliens, he said.

On September 3, he went out for a drive only to find that one of the aliens was in the car with him, he said. Spurred on by the creature, he said he led as many as 10 law enforcement officers on a wild chase through Berryville and Clarke County at speeds exceeding 110 m.p.h.

"At one point I was doing 110 and I couldn't hold a candle to him," said a Berryville town policeman who eventually stopped Turner and charged him with two counts of reckless driving and two counts of failure to heed a siren and flashing lights.

Turner is scheduled to stand trial on the charges November 14. His defense undoubtedly will be the most unusual in the history of the Clarke County General District Court.

Meanwhile, Turner said he is trying to deal with the thought that he should end his life, with the ringing in his ears, and with the messages of warning that come to him unexpectedly from the aliens.

He reads the Bible for some sign of meaning and frets over the sensation that there is something he has been ordered to locate within the next year. There is a symbol of some sort that looks like the numeral "7" with lines drawn through it.

There have been numerous crank calls, "but most of my friends are trying to understand what happened," he said. "They've been good about trying to help me." Efforts to elicit interest from scientific agencies have been unsuccessful.

So he sits at home, mulling it over and over again, smoking and taking pills to calm his nerves.

"Twenty years from now, I'll still probably never know what happened that night," he said, pulling on a religious pendant that has become his only talisman against the forces of his alleged serial-numbered enemies

TRIP AROUND THE WORLD IN A UFO

The UFO saga of Oscar Magocsi was told to me personally while Oscar was vacationing in the United States. He had telephoned me from his Canadian residence and after giving me a brief run down on what had been happening to him over the course of several years, I invited him to stop in and give me a full accounting. Though his story is among the most "wild," he seemed sincere and not the type of individual to be making all this up.

Before my encounter, I had never been a believer in UFOs whatsoever. And I believe now that my first encounter was more or less accidental, and from then on, I had become deeply interested in the UFO phenomenon.

When the first incident took place, I had been in Canada, north of Toronto, a small town near Huntsville — I have vacation property out there. It was at night, and I was sitting outside, near my campfire. And that's where it happened, where I had the first, the very first sighting of my life.

It happened in 1975. I was camping out. I was by myself and as I was sitting by the campfire, it was quiet and I had this strange kind of feeling that something was watching me. I looked up and about 400 yards away I saw this strange object hovering above the tree line. It was a UFO - a flying saucer. After hovering there for awhile, it took off, making no sound at all. It was kind of disc-shaped, it was changing colors, from a yellow-green to orange, and then it started to fluctuate. As it was fluctuating, I felt as though someone - or something - was probing me, trying to read my thoughts. It was almost physical, the feeling. I knew somehow that it was probing into my brain.

At that point I was more curious than frightened. During the next few days I spoke with a few neighbors who happened to be around, trying to bring up the subject casually. I asked if they had ever seen anything strange around these parts. Negative. Nothing. I went around the city of Toronto, asking all kinds of questions, going to lectures. I was interested in the subject. That's when I had bumped into somebody who steered me to an alien contact. That is, one day I went to a UFO lecture, and after the lecture was over, I was approached by one fellow and he said he felt I had something to do with UFOs. "You're linked, or connected, with them," he said. I asked how he knew this, and he answered that he felt this mentally. He said he saw some kind of a symbol around me, an aura, an orange glow. He was a psychic. He picked it up.

I just smiled because I wanted to hear about his experiences, and he told me that something happened to him in the 1960's in California. There had been a major earthquake there, and he was driving to Los Angeles at that time, and he saw a UFO in the sky. He looked up, and the UFO started to fluctuate, glow - orangeish - and his car stalled, just before a bridge spanning a valley. And within a few seconds after the car stalled the bridge collapsed. He told me that the UFOnauts saved his life. From that time on, he was deeply hooked. I didn't really take him seriously. He talked of a blonde stranger, tall, unusual looking. He felt this individual was an alien. I at the time didn't have any comment to make, but a few days later, I wanted to go out to a movie. As I was going down one of the main streets, I stopped to look at a poster on a wall. The poster said something about a psychic fair being held at the Sheraton Hotel. I thought I might go later on, but not this particular evening as I had already made plans to go to the movies. So I flagged down a cab, and I told the driver where I wanted to go.

He didn't take me to the movies. Instead, he took me down to the psychic fair, to the UFO section. I was surprised. I told him, "Didn't I tell you I wanted to go to the movies?" He turned around and grinned. I 'as suspicious of him, and later on I bumped into him in the course of my journey. It was obvious to me that he was an "agent" on a mission. He knew I was going out of the house and he wanted me to go to the Psychic Fair.

Once at the Fair, I bumped into this guy - this tall, blonde stranger. He sort of picked me out of the crowd. I told him about my UFO experience and he told me about the general background of the UFOs. I told him that I would like to have a direct experience, not just a sighting, but something serious. He said, "Well, next summer, in the same area that you had your sighting, around the end of July, that would be the best time. "

He called himself Quenton. He didn't even introduce himself. I just learned this in a round-about way. Later on, I met him again. So, up until the time of the Psychic Fair, I had a couple of sightings in the same area for three consecutive nights. Therefore, this fellow told me that if I go up come summer (this was in February), I'd have a better chance. He was consulting some sort of timetable. I didn't take him seriously, although I had a positive feelings about him. He had lots of charisma. He was youngish, early 30s. He was a very good-looking fellow, like some kind of a super movie star, tall forehead. I guess that's how one would depict an intelligent alien. Good vibes, friendly, he spoke good English.

Come July of 1975, I took my vacation. I went up to the area and I camped out. The first few nights nothing happened, and the second or third night, comes the UFO. It landed behind the hill. I took off on foot with my flashlight and I found it. It was in a forest clearing, on one of the logging roads - a natural clearing, rocky terrain - it was sheer rock, that's why the police couldn't go there. So - I spotted it, it was almost hovering about 60 feet above the ground, almost landing. I stopped about 50 feet from it; and it slowly came down and landed. No noise. I waited for a while, came up close, no doors - nothing. Three portholes, that I had seen, were equally set apart and had a yellowing light coming through them. I couldn't see in because it was higher than my eye level. Then I heard a sound, kind of an air braking sound like you hear on trucks or buses. This made me rush back into the trees. Then I saw a door opening slowly like the iris of a camera. A ramp was lowered as I waited and watched. I figured aliens would be coming out. But nobody appeared. Finally I said to myself that since nobody is coming out, why don't I go and take a look and see what's going on. So, I just walked in. I was scared, frightened, but I felt that if I walked away I'd never know, I'd never learn anything.

I walked inside and there was no one inside at all, no human being or any other kind of an individual. I saw these benches, vertical, semi-circular in shape. There was also this tubing or shaft that was flickering with lights. My impression was that it was some kind of super brain. It was biological. It wasn't just a mass of jelly or flesh, yet it wasn't electrical either. Perhaps it was something in between; sometimes I thought it was a great eye. Or a great brain. It's almost impossible to describe, but it was flickering with all kinds of light patterns. I figured it must be the center of intelligence as it was the only light in the craft.

There were two slats on either side of the craft, I call them instrument slats. No knobs on it. It was transparent, and behind the transparency, all kinds of lights. The room was about 25 feet in diameter and about 10 feet tall. Just enough head room for me. I was on board the craft for just a few minutes. While I was inside, the door closed behind me and I thought I was trapped. I tried to get out. I looked around and I couldn't find the door, it was kind of sealed, seamlessly, and there was a pencil-thin vertical shaft of light nearby. I figured this was kind of a photocell.

I put my rubberized flashlight through the light and the door opened. I got out and went back in again. I did this several times. I just wanted to reassure myself that I could open the door. Next time, I went inside, and stayed to look around more closely. I panicked when this vertical shaft started to energize, almost like streams of water pouring down, like a shower, multi-colored, almost like an energy discharge. I figured that it had something to do with the drive, the propulsion system, but it had no rockets. No propellers or anything…this was around midnight.

When it started to energize, the light began to get more and more intense. It was fluorescent. There were no light fixtures. The whole thing started to glow thicker and thicker. So I panicked, and I got out. I couldn't take anymore. Afterwards, the thing - the ship - just closed up and went away. That was for that night.

A couple of nights later it came again. But I stayed on the property. The next day I got my nerve back. I sort of talked the whole thing out, and I figured I was stupid to have run away. I said to myself, next time, if it comes, I'll stay inside. So, the next time, it landed, the doors opened, I walked in, the door closes and at this time I began to study everything in greater detail. I was inside for about an hour. I said to myself this time if it starts to energize, I won't run away because I'd like to go for a ride.

Then it started to energize, and as it (I guess) picked up my voice, it started to lift. We lifted up to about 1,000 feet first, and I looked through the portholes, I looked down and grabbed this railing. As I grabbed it, I felt as though I had been looking into a zoom lens. It had a magnified effect, an enlargement effect. The whole landscape was almost fully lit although it was pitch black, nighttime. I could see everything.

We flew over to Toronto, which is about 120 miles away in a very, very short time, about 2-3 minutes. Then, from Toronto, (I said, it would be nice if we could go a little bit further) we went over the ocean (10 minutes), we went over to New York City. My watch stopped, so I couldn't check it on my watch, but it took about 10 minutes to get here. Then I said, I wonder what comes next and a thought came into my mind - lets go to the pyramids. I wasn't quite sure whether this was my idea on whether this was put into my mind. Anyway, we flew across the Atlantic to Egypt.

I dozed off for a while, and when I woke up we were right over the great pyramids in Egypt. We were lined up in such a way that the sun was vertical and the apex of the great pyramid was with us and the sun, from the apex of the pyramids was shining right through the tube or window. Some kind of strange energy was flowing right out of the apex of the pyramids into the craft itself. It was sucking up like a vacuum cleaner. We then flew to the Middle East, landing in the desert; I figured it was Syria or those parts.

We waited for a while, I didn't know for what. I went to the door, walked out, and said to myself that there was a dust storm coming closer. It turned out that it wasn't a dust storm, but a column of tanks. As they got closer they started to shoot real heavy artillery. The shells were exploding while I was away a little distant from the saucer, but we were in some kind of a force field that kept the shells out. The closest shell exploded about 40 feet. I just rushed right back to the craft because it was so hot out there, as though I were inside a furnace. The doors closed and we lifted up. The air inside the craft was normalized within seconds. So, we lifted up, and about 10,000 feet altitude or so we encountered fighters, interceptors, coming close. Three planes in formation. They were Arab planes I think. I wasn't sure because they were flashing by within seconds, so fast. I just couldn't see the insignia. The lead plane fired two missiles. Then the saucer lifted up so fast I thought my stomach was left back in the desert.

While we were lifting up, I saw those two missiles curbing after us. I felt we were in trouble, but the saucer used two beams of light which I saw issuing forth, like a laser cannon, and destroyed them from half- a- mile away. The planes, of course, were already gone. I felt somehow that all this was done purposely - the saucer wanting to show its defense capabilities. So then we flew to Tibet, the Himalayas and we landed some-place high in the mountains. Not down in the valley, but close to the peaks, at a very desolate place. So we stopped there and were sitting there for a while, how long I don't know. We saw this line of people coming by, carrying torches. They looked like monks who live up in the mountains.

One of these guys comes up to the saucer. They were carrying torches because the sun had already set. One of them, as I said, comes up to the saucer, opening the door - evidently he knew how - and sees me and throws over a pair of funny boots and motions for me to put it on. So I did, and he said, "Come on," and they escorted me from the saucer into the mountains through funny underground caves and into an underground monastery, which was full of funny- looking monks. The funny thing was the faces were not only Oriental, but lots of white faces and black faces, and red Indian faces - it seemed that everybody from all over the world was represented.

I sat down in a chair in a circle of monks. They were chanting and incense was burning and they were sort of scrutinizing me, in what I felt was some kind of religious festival. Then I dozed off for a while and at one point I thought I saw the old man, or head Lama, seated opposite me. And as I was looking at him he was rising up from his chair. Levitating. Then the whole area just opened up so that I could see the whole valley and the saucer hovering nearby, with its orange glow. The next minute I found myself standing out on a balcony, or a terrace with the head Lama. It was very cold. Then these other guys escorted me back to the saucer. I got in, and we crossed the Atlantic and went to South America - Chile - that area. Oh, yes, in Tibet, when we took off, it was sunrise, very early morning. When we flew over the Atlantic, heading towards South America, the sun was coming up again.

When we reached the west coast of South America, it was late afternoon, and so we kept circling until the sun went down. I had seen lightning bolts issuing from the mountains. It was coming from down below. It was aimed at the saucer as though they were shooting lightning bolts at us. Greenish lightning bolts. We just flew away and came to California - northern California.

I figured that it must have been Mount Shasta. So, we went to the top of the mountain and from the apex, looking down, I saw three campfires lit up. I saw guys around the fires, and then the saucer discharged some kind of energy right into the mountain's peak, like a big shower. And then we went away, and that's it.

We landed in the same spot that I was originally picked up. The entire experience lasted 23 hours. I went around the world in a UFO in 23 hours. Insofar as being tired from the trip is concerned, I was. And insofar as the food, I found a cubicle I managed to open and found storage - cubes, condensed food. And I found water. That was my first trip. I was happy after that. So, a few days later, the saucer comes again to the same spot and lands, and I got into it and went on another trip. This time we went interdimensional — into another dimension.

I found a space suit laid out for my use, which I put on. Actually, it was much like a skin divers suit, silvery on the outside and lined on the inside. It had a belt, a wide belt, and like a motorcycle helmet.

At that point we were hovering over Lake Ontario, roughly between Toronto and Niagara Falls. Still, I hadn't at this point met anybody on the ship. Anyway, I was looking through the porthole, at the skyline of Toronto, the lit buildings and all of a sudden I was in deep space. It was another dimension. A parallel. But at that point I didn't know this. Later on I learned about it in a round about way, and I was told, by the one I met at the Psychic Fair.

"They are from another dimension altogether. They accidentally stumbled into ours, and there are quite a number of other dimensions interconnected," he said. He called his world the Psychician Federation of Worlds. He was a psychician. The saucer could fade in and out from our world to theirs, but it has to stay there for only a few seconds because it can not transfer over completely, but as I said, only for a few seconds from the radar screen.

So we faded back into Earth's dimension and we flew away towards Florida this time. Jacksonville, going towards the ocean. It was dark. We went into a vortex, and it was dark and then we came out of it somehow. Nearby there was a craft waiting for us. It was some kind of mother ship, a saucer carrier. They had about seven altogether. Seven babies, you might say. The walls were transparent and we just penetrated through the walls. When we were inside, everything became solid, faded back. Then a door opened, normal air, normal everything, I walked through the door and found myself inside. There was a huge dome in the center. It was like a rock garden, or a jungle, an area for recreation, just for walking around. You know, I saw nobody else because they wanted to keep us anonymous from each other, for I think there were more people like me they picked up. But I didn't see anybody. I think they wanted for us to seek each other out, later on, wherever we may be. There were seven ships in all, and I think seven people in all.

In any event, after two or three days of space flight, we landed on a planet, called Argona, which had a binary system, two sides, one was called Om and the other Um. Argona of the Om Um system. This was one of the planets of the Psychician Federation of Worlds. I communicated with people when I was there. There was a reception center and the people looked human. That's where I bumped into the guy who originally took me to the psychic fair. He might have been a cab driver, but I suspected him to be an alien. During my time on this far distant planet, this man was my host. He took me around this planet on more-or-less of a tour of both the city and of their countryside.

The city was domed in, with a lot of tall structures like skyscrapers but not exactly the same. The whole planet was only recreational. The reception committee spoke English to me. But the rest of the people with whom I was rubbing elbows, the thousands and thousands of people, they didn't even know who I was. They were from all kinds of other systems. They looked weird to me, but I must have looked weird to them. There were so many different skin colors and dresses and heights and what not, that some of them were looking facially like a cat or dog or frog, or whatever. Actually, they did speak some common language. It resembled a Chinese singsong to my ear.

Upon my arrival, the reception committee took me to their center that had been specially constructed for visitors. It was furnished like any earth place to make a guy feel at home. Inside the center at the time they had about a dozen people who were from various dimensions and galaxies. They were on a common mission. That mission was to be trained in earth mannerisms and earth languages so that they could be sent down here to do whatever they were supposed to do. They were supposed to speak freely with earth people, to pass for normal human beings.

They had common names like George or Joe, and were said to be from Japan or China. One woman said she was from New York City, but in reality she had never even been to earth before. Before she was set to come to Earth, and she knew already all the mannerisms, even played the piano.

At any given time, I figured there must be dozens if not hundreds of people for various purposes. It's not very likely that any of these people would ever be detected, except, very likely, by psychic means. But they looked much nicer, more handsome than we are. They looked more intelligent. There were subtle things about them, that you could pick them out for instance, little things. Somebody may know New York City, but they wouldn't know how to get to 57th street. Small things. It's very likely that this girl I met there, who knew New York - she called herself Melody, she could be here right now. She was a gorgeous looking redhead. And she sings.

Mainly, the purpose of their interest is that they are greatly concerned about our whole life nature, and about our vibrations, as they call it, our emanations which are causing psychic pollution in the air. It's causing, almost like smog, the psychic pollution which comes out of bad vibes.

All the crises and problems in the world is contaminating the earth's psychic atmosphere, in such a bad way, that we would get into a nuclear war and wipe ourselves out. It seems they are greatly concerned. Very much. They wouldn't stop us from wiping ourselves out. That's a no-no. If we want to blow ourselves up, that's fine. But should that happen, they are willing to rescue quite a very few people from here. Selections will be done through aura. They have aura detectors. I understand that if you are in a bad mood one day and in a good mood the next day, your aura does change. But that's on the surface only.

They're interested in what kind of an attitude you have socially, spiritually, psychically. These things take years and years and do not change overnight. Anyway, these people will be rescued in space shuttles, capable of taking on board thousands of people. Space arcs, they're called. So they could rescue quite a lot. They would take them to an artificial planet in an almost halfway dimension. It's already there, a physical planet. I don't know how many exactly would be rescued. They didn't say.

Of course, if one country shoots off a missile, and another country retaliates, it will be over quite fast. But they were talking about survivors, whoever happens to survive. And as a consequence of nuclear war, they are talking about natural catastrophes. For many, many years through various channels, they have been educating people about this, what might be coming, and what they are prepared to do in the event — rescue who's left. Whenever the time may be right, they said, war, catastrophe and the like notwithstanding, one day, they would like to show themselves openly. In the near future, they said, there will be a public landing. Whenever the time may be right. They can't do it now because history would change course, we would never be the same. I suspect they talked already with government leaders about this, but they didn't say. Insofar as contact is concerned, sporadically, I do have contact. Nothing on an organized level scale. When they want to, they get in touch with me. The last time they got in touch with me was a year ago in August, down in Indiana. I suspect that in a few weeks time, they will get in touch with me again. In Indiana, I ran into a bunch of people at a convention, from Camp Chesterfield, and I felt many of them were aliens. I was invited down by some friends. At that time I wasn't carrying a camera with me, but now I am.

Anyway, after my contact, I didn't want to tell just anybody about it. I'm kind of a private person. Later on, when I decided to write the story, I did. It took roc about two years to write down the whole thing. I think the reason that I was taken onboard was because they wanted to pick a few specimens, just an average, ordinary Joe, and I happened to be at the right place at the right time. They evidently wanted to see how the average guy looks, feels about things, reacts.

I was at the reception center for about three days. But it was very intensive. I was with them day and night. Like in a laboratory. That was my feeling anyway. They wanted to see my physical coordination, how fast I was on the uptake. I feel they are very advanced technologically than ourselves, many thousands of years, perhaps even millions. But it's very hard to figure because we don't know how far advanced we will be in a hundred year's time. But we could never catch up with them even in one hundred thousand year's time. Insofar as the council of planets are concerned, there must be thousands of other planets who belong. The whole idea is that in time, to accept us in it.

Contact, they said, will eventually have to be made with us, because there are other space going species from various other parts who are negative beings, from various other parts of the universe. They wouldn't want those negative beings to get us first. Because we could be used as dupes as a weapon against the friendly ones. So, they would want to help us as much as possible, protect us from the unfriendly ones that are loose.

They didn't discuss the MIB, the Men In Black, these negative beings, but I had a few run ins with them. Once I found a note - it was a cutout from a newspaper, about someone who published a book on UFOs and who disappeared. I found this cutout in my locked car - on the inside. I don't know how the hell they got in to put it there. I feel that was a hint. But I wouldn't let myself worry about that. Insofar as some of the other contact stories I'd heard about, I think there must be something to it, because the universe is so big and there are so many space going species. Last year, as you undoubtedly know, TV was taken over by the extraterrestrials. As time goes on, these things are going to happen more and more, so that many millions of people will hear them.

Anyway, these beings are being directed, governed, by beings that are higher, from an even higher dimension, by beings who aren't flesh and blood, like energy beings, spiritual beings, who are called the Council for the Hierarchy. We spoke of philosophy. They asked me questions and I asked them questions. I asked them, "Do you know God?" They said, "No, nobody does. The cosmos is so vast," they said, "that there is no answer. Everyone has to find his own answer."

A parting note: there must be a way to get more harmony here on Earth, but I don't know how to go about it. All this has changed my life. I have a much wider horizon now. I became much more psychic. There's more to life, I realize now, than eat, sleep and be merry. I would like to contact other beings on the other levels of existence. Some of these spiritualists maintain that they get their stuff from the spirit of somebody's deceased grandmother.

When I proved to them my own psychic development, they asked; "Where is your stuff coming from?" I said, "I haven't got any bloody proof. But it's not important," I told them. "I just pick these things up." In all though, I spent a total of seven days with these entities.

Here I am on the set of the *UFO Hunters* shooting an episode that aired under the title of *The Silencers* (it's posted on YouTube). It was about my encounter with a man in black in Jersey City. We shot the scene in Arizona. Go figure.

CHAPTER THREE: STRANGE ALIENS FROM SPACE AND TIME

NOT all UFOnauts are golden-haired Venusians or little men with bluish-gray skin. Occasionally, a door opens somewhere in our atmosphere and some unusual entities decide to drop in. This story, written by Carol Wahlen of the Northeast (Wisconsin) Post, is a good example of such a case that certainly gave me the creeps when I first heard of it, and it will probably give you a shiver or two.

STRANGE VISITORS UPSET TOSA COUPLE

Are people from outer space visiting our planet?

Anne and Peter E. of Wauwatosa think they are. In fact, they believe they had such visitors last year.

Pete, 64, who was a foreman with a local construction company for over 30 years until his retirement in 1973, still gets excited when he speaks of the experience.

Anne, 59, says she wouldn't believe it if she hadn't seen it herself.

It was in November, the tenth to be exact. Pete remembered the date as if it were branded on his memory. The doorbell rang at 7:50 p.m. Anne, going to answer the bell, peeped through the curtained window on the door as was her usual practice. Standing just below the stoop, about four feet from the door, was a strangely dressed person of average height. He was grasping a five foot white staff with his left hand.

Opening the inner door, Anne quickly locked the screen door; even though it was November, Pete hadn't put on the storm door because it had been a mild fall and the cold Wisconsin winter hadn't arrived.

"Yes?" Anne asked through the screen door. Hearing no reply, she again said. "Yes?"

At this point, she turned to her husband for assistance. "Come here, he doesn't talk," she said.

Pete went to the door. Upon seeing the strange looking person, he remarked, "What the hell is this, something left over from trick or treat?" With that, Pete unlocked the screen door and opened it in order to get a better look. The lights from the house clearly lit the visitor.

"The skin on his face was the same as smoked meat and the face was lined with deep grooves," Pete said. He went on to describe the stranger's mouth as a small puckered opening, no bigger than a dime. Other than recalling that the visitor had a very pointed chin, Pete could not remember any other facial features.

Anne also drew a blank when it came to describing the rest of the visitor's face but she did remember his hat. "It was shaped like a man's straw hat except the brim was narrower," she recalled. Pete added another item to the description; the person had tufts of hair sticking out from either side of the hat. He could not remember the color of the hair.

As Pete leaned out to grab what he at first thought was a prankster, the visitor raised his white staff and rapped it on the sidewalk. The staff made three clicking sounds and the stranger moved away. "He didn't step back or jump back, he just drifted away from me," Pete said. It was then that Pete became aware of four other creatures out on the lawn and in the street. "They were all dressed alike and they all carried a white staff in their left hands," Pete said. "One of them was heavier than the rest. He was out in the middle of the street. He was rapping his staff on the asphalt and floating two to three feet above the ground each time it clicked. The staff seemed to be some kind of an energy stick. That roly-poly one seemed to be having the time of his life, bouncing up and down like that. He looked like the astronauts looked when they jumped on the moon, only he seemed to have more control over his movements than they did."

Pete described the other three visitors as just moving across the lawn. "Their feet were making walking motions but they were two or three inches above the ground," he said excitedly. All of them, he said, had a deformed look. He described their hands as looking like arthritic claws and their legs as being bent and bowed. "They looked like over-sized gnomes," he said. "As I leaned out, Anne grabbed hold of the suspenders on my overalls and pulled. When she got me back inside the house, I couldn't remember much about their faces or dress," Pete said. "As I fell into a chair, Anne looked out the front window," he said.

"I could see only three of them," Anne said. "The one that had been at the door was drifting across the lawn. He turned and raised his hand to me. It wasn't a clenched fist, just kind of bent, that's how all their hands we're naturally."

Both Pete and his wife agreed that they did not feel threatened by the visitors. As to why they came to his house, Pete could not give a reason. He thought that their way of communicating was probably different from ours because their mouths were so much smaller. He wondered if they could eat with such a small opening and concluded that maybe they could drink liquids through a straw.

As soon as he regained his composure, Pete called the Wauwatosa Police Department. Officer Daniel Anderson, after receiving a radio message about strange looking people annoying residents on Beverly Place, surveyed the area around the Menomonee River Parkway. The Parkway is two blocks from the home.

Pete called the police the next day and the day after that to see if the police had found anything.

On the third day, Officer Anderson came to the house to say that he had found nothing. Anne and Pete said they got the impression that Anderson thought that they were a couple of nuts.

Apparently, that must have been the officer's opinion because he did not write up a report about the incident.

Pete and Anne still believe they were visited by spacemen even though they have had to take a lot of kidding from friends and relatives. "My own son walks hunchbacked and says click-click just to kid us," Pete said. Only one neighbor has been receptive to the story. He and his wife saw a strange vehicle in the sky while driving through the Menomonee River Parkway two years ago. His neighbors never told anyone about it until now because they were afraid people would make fun of them.

"You know they were right. No one takes us seriously. They all think we are making it up or that someone pulled a joke on us. I'll believe it was a joke when someone shows me those staffs," Pete said.

"Besides, the whole thing took about two minutes. Who would go to so much trouble for just two minutes? And how could anyone get people to float all over my lawn?"

Now here's an even odder report from two Delaware men who swear on the Bible that they saw a couple of 9-foot tall Martians hugging in a field. Check the *Milford Chronicle* for December 9, 1976 if you don't believe this happened.

NINE FOOT "MARTIANS"

Two Milford men are shaking their heads this week and swearing it happened - they say they saw an Unidentified Flying Object outside town last weekend.

John Brady and Ronald Fullman swear they saw the UFO or the occupants from one, as they returned home last Monday morning from Milton.

"We ordinarily come up the highway, but we decided to come the back way," Brady explains. "We were coming through Slaughter Neck and we stopped at the stop sign by the Milford by-pass."

Brady says that when they stopped at the road sign, he glanced over into the cornfield next to the road. He swears he saw "two tall objects, maybe eight or nine feet tall, standing close together as though they were hugging."

The sight of it shocked him so much he looked over at his companion and Fullman was staring at the same thing. Fullman even opened his car door to make sure they were truly seeing something outside the car, according to Brady. There were no lights about the figures or luminescence to them, but Brady says the night was very bright and it was easy to see. He described the objects as green-looking, "sort of a pine green."

"We went back to the same spot Monday," he relates. "We both agreed on the location where 'they' were standing. It was about 100 yards off the highway in the cornfield.

"There were no trees there and no machinery that might have confused us. We looked for prints on the ground or some other mark to show something had been there but we couldn't find a thing. We even took some of our friends back to look at the spot.

"There's no doubt in my mind that something was there," Brady swore Tuesday. "People will think we're crazy but we know we saw something."

He estimated the sighting happened about 3:30 a.m.

If you thought "Flower Power" was only big in the 1960's, you are wrong. A Florida woman says she encountered some mighty peculiar aliens over a half century ago while she was growing up. *The Weekday*, a paper published in West Palm Beach gives all the details.

* * *

FLOWER PEOPLE IN UFO SAID . . .

Mrs. Evelyn Wendt has carried a secret for the past fifty years. In 1924, she saw and talked to people from a UFO.

"But in all that time, I've never said much about it. You have no idea what I went through in those days. People used to laugh and think I was crazy," the beauty salon operator explained. "Even my husband - well I'd rather not talk about it."

Now, however, the friendly woman in her middle years feels that times have changed. "This is only the second time I've talked about the experience. Times have changed," Mrs. Wendt smiled.

The event took place while Evelyn was playing in the schoolyard of the Holy Name Convent School in Dade City, Florida. "The UFO must have knocked me out, because the first thing I remember is that this egg-shaped thing was on the ground, and this bright light was shining in my eyes," Mrs. Wendt recounted. "Then the light went out, and a hatch opened from the upper edge to the ground. Little people emerged. I think they were robots. I tried to count them, but they charged about so. They were smaller than I was, and resembled animated flowers with faces where the bud would be. Remember, I was just a bitty thing then, and kids don't fear flowers."

The little people were carrying a weapon of some sort to the school's science building, Mrs. Wendt continued. "I wanted to help them, but someone said 'stop.' I replied they were so small and I was going to assist. They let me try, but I couldn't even budge the machine. "I was told they were going to stop the work that was being done in the science building and they said if the work continued, they would destroy the place." Asked what the "work" was, Mrs. Wendt shook her head. "All I know is later I heard the place was a shambles.

"There seemed to be a man with the little people," Mrs. Wendt added. "Everything looked real, even though I wasn't so sure. The conversation wasn't real talking," the auburn-haired lady continued, but she knew inside somehow, what was being said.

"Later, when the people were going to leave, they asked if I wanted to go. I said 'no', but I could have gone," Mrs. Wendt said. "They promised to come back for me in thirty five years, but that was up a long time ago and nothing happened that I know of," Mrs. Wendt laughed shortly.

"Just recently when I told my story to a Mr. Stephen Putnam from the scientific organization investigating UFOs, he said the group is trying to duplicate the UFO propulsion and verify the reported sightings. He also said he knew my sighting was valid because of certain parts in my story that are the same as many other true happenings."

Asked what those specific parts were Mrs. Wendt shook her head.

"I can't tell you what those facts were. It would not be a good idea for everyone to know." She also added that the scientist had not forbidden any sort of disclosure.

"Mr. Putnam also took me to a hypnotist to check out my story in that manner, but for some reason I wasn't able to be hypnotized," Mrs. Wendt said in a puzzled manner.

The Riviera Beach resident added, however, that if anyone provided the funds for another attempt at hypnosis, she would be willing to cooperate.

"All I can remember now is that the saucer was leaden-looking and very pock-marked. Then, when it started up its molecules expanded and it turned silvery bright. The UFO then went straight up, hovered a minute and disappeared from my sight."

* * *

Thumbing through some old files I found a yellowed clipping dated Sunday, September 30, 1973 that had been clipped from *THE ROBESONIAN*, Lumberton, N.C. by a veteran UFOlogist, George D. Fawcett. The story by staff writer Lee Hamilton concerns a UFOnaut that would scare anyone to the bone.

"SPACE MONSTER" REPORTS CREATE UPROAR IN TABOR CITY VICINITY

The crossroads community of Sydney, just out of Tabor City on the Whiteville Road, has been a rather quiet, sleepy little village ... until early last week that is.

Suddenly and without warning, Sydney found itself under the harsh glare of statewide headlines and TV lights when it became the focus of reports of a seven-to-eight-foot tall "creature," said to be wandering about in the wooded areas surrounding the community.

Thursday night, it was quiet - or relatively calm, at any rate - for the sudden influx Wednesday night of hundreds of sightseers, the crack of rifles and the advent of law enforcement authorities seemed to have hustled the "space monster" back into the obscurity of the woods or out of the area altogether.

Those who say they have seen it, however, are not to be convinced otherwise, and stick with their stories no matter how much they are made the subject of ridicule by others who have been there but have seen nothing.

Miss Williamson, one of the first to report the sighting of the alien visitor, has been subsequently jailed in lieu of $2,000 bond, and charged with shooting firearms into a public area according to Sheriff Ben Duke.

She is accused of firing a shotgun at "the elusive space monster" on several occasions during the past week.

Her hearing in district court is upcoming on October 11. Miss Williamson, who said that she, her father and her sister had been harassed since last week by not one, but two of the creatures, called Ken Williamson (no relation), a radio deejay for WTAB in Tabor City, saying that she had to have some relief."

Ken, with three friends, went to the site, and reported that they too saw the creature.

Deejay Williamson, along with Glen Bryant and Dennie Floyd of Green Sea, S.C., and Miss Gayle Sarvis of Tabor City, said they drove out to Sydney about 12:30 a.m. Tuesday, contacted Miss Williamson, and then looked around the wooded area.

He said that "... Miss Williamson shined a flashlight into a clearing — and T thought I saw a face."

The radioman drew a sketch of what he thought he saw, which the other three corroborated.

The description, according to the various witnesses, states that the entity is from seven to eight feet tall, with red or orange eyes (oblong), pointed ears, and a face that looks as though it is made of scored reddish-brown modeling clay.

Not everyone has experienced a sighting, as it were, for another friend of Williamson's, Dean Graham, also of Green Sea, who was not with the original group but who has been to the area several times, says that he has yet to see anything.

Thursday night, all that could be discovered around Sydney was something of a minor traffic jam, someone shooting firecrackers, and several darkened houses and service stations, and quite a bit of dust hanging in the air.

Deejay Williamson, at the radio station Thursday night, said that he was not planning to go back to the site again, adding that he had seen enough. Pointing to a loaded .22 caliber revolver on his desk at the station, he stated emphatically that he wasn't taking any chances on it (the creature) coming to visit him either.

Some reports stressed that the being left no footprints, indicating that it never actually touched the ground, but hovered a few inches away from the surface. It was also said to be able to leap effortlessly from 60 to 100 feet in a horizontal direction.

Another witness said that it was seen drinking water from a car radiator; while yet another person, referring to its attire, spoke of a ragged, camouflage-type shirt and ragged black pants with brogan-type shoes studded with rhinestone-like adornment or an array of silver eyelets.

Miss Williamson stated that the sound that it made was something of a high-pitched or high frequency squeak.

The deejay admitted firing at the monster, but added that it "... didn't do anything ... but about a minute later, it just shimmered out and disappeared."

According to Sheriff Duke, there were several reports of shots being fired at the creatures, and that buckshot had struck a camper parked in one nearby yard.

Although some 200 curiosity-seekers and monster-hunters showed up on Wednesday night, the sheriff said, they cooperated when asked to move on by deputies at the scene.

Williamson said that cars were parked along the road for "quite a ways" in both directions around Sydney on Wednesday night, and that parking tickets were being handed out "by the dozens."

Sheriff Duke later said that his deputies had found no tangible evidence whatsoever of monsters in the area. "We have looked for tracks and had the bloodhounds in there," he added, "but there was nothing found."

There are some who want to connect the recent sighting by Charleston, S.C. police officers of several UFOs over that city with the recent events at Sydney, but neither incident has been confirmed by official sources.

Whatever it was that the numerous - and very serious – witnesses saw, it surely has set that section of Columbus County into an uproar.

In the same folder I found this story from the Danville (VA.) Bee dated October 19 of the same year. Another monster and only a state or so away. Too close for comfort I'd say!

UFO "THING" CHASES BOYS ON WHITE OAK

Some Danville citizens, not to be outdone by the recent rash of UFO sightings across the nation, are now reporting seeing things in the crisp, clear autumn skies.

Early last evening on White Oak Mountain, just south of Chatham, Bill Hines, a Guilford St. youth, and his friend told Danville police they were chased by a bright white "thing" which was three to four feet tall.

The boys said this "thing" with a shimmering body, had a large head with no eyes, and ran sideways.

They related that they ran back to a pickup truck where an adult was waiting for them. The report did not say if the adult also saw the "thing."

Just after they reached the apparent safety of the truck, a green, hazy cloud was seen moving up and away into the sky, headed north.

Police added that about this same time state troopers in Salem reported seeing a red ball of fire in the sky, "believe it or not."

Adding a note of further mystery to the story, Mrs. Pat Wentz of Laramie Circle had reported to police earlier that she had seen a UFO, which looked like a "bright star" in the night sky over the Old Mayfield Rd. She said it disappeared toward White Oak Mountain.

Along with the police report of the incident came a suggestion not to laugh too soon - a number of other area residents also saw this bright light in the sky at the same time Mrs. Wentz reported the sighting.

A few days later the residents of Hartford City, Indiana must have wondered what was going on when they read the following story carried in the *Muncie Star* on October 24. My, those aliens certainly get around.

SILVERY MIDGETS

Two silver-plated midgets with powers of flight visited eastern Blackford County late Monday and early Tuesday, according to several residents, who say they saw the weird-looking "spacemen" jumping up and down near Ind. 26.

Gary Flatter, R.R.2, told *The Star* he watched two four-foot tall silvery things in a cornfield shortly after 1 a.m. Tuesday for about three minutes before the visitors flew away.

DeWayne Donathon, R.R.I, reported to the sheriff's department he and his wife almost struck the pair with their car on Ind. 26. According to Donathon, the strange visitors were hopping up and down in the road and barely managed to scurry off the highway in time to avoid being hit.

Flatter said he saw two "short things, about four-feet tall, with gas-mask-like masks on their heads" on the north side of Ind. 26 east of here. He said the little men had oblong heads and rectangular feet and moved with difficulty, "like robots."

Flatter, who owns Chaney's Corner Wrecking Service, was driving his wrecker around the area looking for unidentified flying objects that had been reported in the area. Deputy Sheriff Ed Townsend was working with Flatter driving his patrol car in the opposite direction. Townsend said he was investigating reports of the undersized men that had been received from Donathon and another unidentified man. The first report was given to Townsend at 9:30 p.m. Monday that two children were out walking along the road, dressed like spacemen.

"In one place we heard and felt this pulsating sound," Townsend said Tuesday. "It was a pulsating, electric feeling ... we could only get it within a couple hundred feet of the place." Flatter described the sound, which he said grew stronger when he saw the silver creatures, as a "high pitched radio wave."

Townsend went back to town about 15 minutes before Flatter saw the little men.

"They were standing about 50 feet on the north-side of the fence (around the cornfield) and just looking at me looking at them. I turned my spotlight on them and the reflection was very bright, something between a reflection from a mirror and a piece of galvanized steel. They had masks on and a tube running into their chests. Their feet were about three-by-six and their hands were just stubs, no fingers that I could see.

"When I shined the light on them they turned away from it, but not like you or I would turn. They just kind of turned all at once, just sort of swiveled, feet and everything. I watched them for about 30 more seconds, then they sort of moved and wiggled their feet and they came up off the ground and they were gone."

Flatter and Townsend returned to the field Tuesday to look for tracks. Townsend said they found footprints with a large, square heel and no toes. Flatter said he would not be anxious to repeat the experience.

UFO researcher Tim R. Swartz, who lived in the nearby town of Elwood at the time, investigated these strange events and spent a good deal of time talking to the witnesses. After checking out the locations, Swartz received information that two local boys had wrapped themselves in aluminum foil and deliberately went out to fool people into thinking that they were "spacemen." It is unknown whether the hoaxers were responsible for every reported incident in the area. However, the witnesses remain convinced that they saw something strange, not two kids out for a joke.

There are plenty of aliens to go around and witnesses of all ages, as this story from *The Review* of Toppenish, Washington, amply testifies. Penned by reporter Frances Story, it appeared on January 26, 1977.

HARRAH YOUTH REPORTS UFOS WITH "GREENISH CREATURES"

Martha Cantu of Harrah said if her son ever tells her again to come and look, she'll be sure to do it. Last Wednesday when her agitated nine-year-old son Jose woke his mother up at about 6:30 a.m. asking her to explain the little "man" he saw outside, she discounted his story and settled down to catch up on the sleep she'd lost the night before with a fussy baby.

Jose, who had been in the middle of preparing his breakfast, wasn't put off so easily. He went outside to check for himself - and came back with an amazing story. He told his mother he had seen two greenish creatures about three feet tall, who rotated on a base instead of having feet, and two "steely" crafts in which two other creatures were sitting.

He claimed that one craft rested in the back yard and the other on a flat section of the roof of the house. He told her he had hidden behind a washing machine stored outside next to a shed. From that vantage point, he said he saw the two creatures join the other two in the crafts. He added that the crafts were brilliantly lighted inside, had "straight stairs" (much like a ramp) and a door that opened in "two parts, like a cross" to reveal the interior which contained two chairs with very tall bases. Jose said the craft in the yard rose from the ground and disappeared into something that resembled a cloud, steam or smoke.

When she heard the story, Jose's mother did what any mother might do in the same circumstances. She sent him to school. At the Harrah Grade School, Jose repeated the story to Diane Gomez, an aide. "Jose is a serious boy. He's not one that tells stories or lies. What he told me, I took very seriously," Gomez said.

At 10:10, recess time, Gomez and another aide accompanied Jose to his home. There he showed them the places where he said the two creatures had been standing. In one location, where Jose said one creature had rotated on his base, Gomez said she saw two round marks in the gravel. At another place, where the creatures allegedly stood, there were two sets of three indentations.

After Mrs. Cantu spoke to the teacher's aides and they had returned to school with Jose, she called her neighbor, Irene Sanchez, to come to her home. Sanchez said they examined the back yard and found in the long grass a circular impression about 10 feet in diameter in which the grass in the middle was whirled up, and observed the marks the aides had seen. The circle was easily visible from the window of the house next door, Gomez said, and added that her brother, who lives there, had seen it from that distance. The circle was still clearly visible when Mr. Cantu arrived home that evening from work, he said.

On Thursday afternoon, when Bill Bogel of Toppenish and David Akers of Seattle, who is affiliated with the Center for UFO Studies, visited the Cantu home, the perfectly shaped circle and "footsteps" were still discernible Akers examined the area with a Geiger counter and got no reaction.

On Saturday when this reporter visited the Cantu home only one set of "foot" marks could still be seen and only a faint trace of the circle remained.

Because the Cantu family is more at home with the Spanish language, this reporter took along a skeptical translator. After he questioned Jose,

who answered his questions seriously and respectfully but asked to be allowed to return to his play, the skeptic concluded that "I believe he saw what he said he saw."

Vogel said he and Akers thought that Jose had "definitely" had an experience with a UFO.

If Jose did, he is in good company. Barbara Brost, co-owner with her husband Earl of the Huba Huba Cafe in Toppenish, had a similar experience 20 years ago in southern Idaho on a ranch east of Blackfoot.

On a summer morning - about 6 a.m. - Barbara and her uncle were saddling horses and, as they left the barn by a rear door, they spotted an object "grayish white and as big as a boxcar" about half a mile away. Stunned, they watched it for about a minute. Barbara's aunt and Earl rushed from the house when the two called to them, but Earl was too late to see the cigar- shaped object which seemed to lift from the ground with a noise "like the transference of air," Barbara said. It disappeared so rapidly she couldn't tell which way it went, she said. "When I see those rockets lift off now, on TV, I just say to myself 'this thing was something else!'"

Another Toppenish resident, a man who prefers not to be identified, made a similar sighting eight years ago over a cornfield in Toppenish. The object that he, his wife, son and daughter saw from a distance of a quarter of a mile or less from their home was "not large. It was huge."

When asked to equate it to the size of a boxcar, he estimated it would be the length of three such train cars. He has described the object, which was off the ground and periodically beaming a light so brilliant that he was unable to look at it without squinting, to a Boeing employee who did his best to convince him that he had not seen the object and, if he had that it was a helicopter. "I know what I saw, "was his answer to that.

At the time, he had a loaded Polaroid camera in his home "but didn't even think of it," he said. The incident raised the "hair on the back of my neck," he said.

A more recent sighting happened in the late fall of 1958 or 1959, about 9 p.m. when Toppenish resident Ron Gardner was living in a rural area. Gardner was about 14 years old at the time. He said he was watching television in the family's long and narrow living room with his back to a picture window in the room. A brilliant, bluish-violet light filled the room, he said. At first he thought it was "an electric arc light." Turning to the window he saw the yard bathed in the purplish light and an object passing about 10 feet from the window. The object, he said was off the ground about three feet, was about seven feet high "tapering to real thin at the bottom," was engulfed in the light and the last four feet of "whatever it was" was disappearing behind a building.

Gardner said his father accused him of watching too many Flash Gordon pictures and he never talked about it very much to anyone but "I know what I saw and I've never seen anything like it since."

Vogel, who seems to be the man in Toppenish to whom all the UFO reports are given, said that there has been many reports of brilliant lights over the Harrah area in the past six to eight months.

He said reports of a bright light over Harrah were made by many CBers the Tuesday night before Jose Cantu claimed to have seen the men and crafts.

A bright light has also been spotted over Toppenish Ridge by Mrs. Stan Johnson of Toppenish, who was Toppenish's Woman of the Year three years ago. She shared the experience with a friend, Judi Farquharson of Toppenish. They reported the lights to the Toppenish Police, who notified Vogel, who watched the light until it disappeared over Union Gap.

The Johnsons, who are area farmers, have seen the light often - and are still trying to explain how three holes, about four feet deep and six feet wide, appeared all in a row in a field in which they were growing sugar beets just south of Harrah.

Those who have seen the lights and mysterious objects all agree that they "know what they saw" but they aren't betting on convincing anyone else of it.

Dr. Wendy M. Lockwood of Sedalia, Colorado, has studied with the "White Brotherhood" for many years. Dr. Lockwood possesses many insights based upon her deep understanding of metaphysics. She says that in any aspect of our physical reality there are both "positive" and "negative" forces attempting to pull us in their direction.

To her way of thinking, not all aliens are Space Brothers. Some, she says, belong to a serpent race that tempted Eve and are now trying to sway our thinking, catching us off balance in a very troubled period in mankind's history. In the special report that follows, Dr. Lockwood describes her own space contacts and tells us how to avoid the trouble spots in attempting to link ourselves with the stars.

THE FORCES OF GOOD AND EVIL

The next time you find yourself in a super market crowd or strolling the corridors of a shopping mall, consider the possibility that you may unknowingly encounter an alien to this planet. The typical alien image is usually undetectable unless one is gifted with inner-sight. There are two basic alien types, each here on a mission to Earth.

One mission is to establish hopeless corruption and darkness, and the other's assignment is to form light and virtue among mankind; to eliminate ignorance by teaching man the riddle of life. Earth is the meeting place and battlefield of those two opposing influences. We are suspended between them and possess the freedom of choice to select whichever side we are drawn toward, according to our inner perceptions.

This is why, especially recently, the New Age movements have stressed the awakening of the sixth sense. Unless the sixth sense is recovered, we may seldom be certain as to whether an alien is harmless or exceedingly dangerous. The time has arrived in history when knowledge of and communication between all planets have been lifted. Previously only those beings who were of the Cosmic Elect qualified to pass those walls. The barriers have been lifted and replaced many times during the past ten million years. This is the last lifting.

Because the Cosmos is nearing it's material end, all intelligences from all dimensions, interlocking spaces and planets must establish enduring harmony with one another as well as the Creator. There is but ONE Creator it is HE who created all things, common and uncommon.

Earth is a prison-world. It is referred to by the Inter-Galactic Voyager as, "THE GREAT TOMB". Why? Because it is the assembly grounds of all Cosmic rebels throughout the entire universe . All who resist peace and order are sent to this world. It is no honor to dwell upon Earth. Those rebels are frequently referred to as "fallen".

They were imprisoned here upon this unilluminated world where they forgot the great knowledge and wisdom they once knew. Their ALL-KNOWING was removed because such rebellious ones could cause great disaster and harm with it.

Down through history, waves of mankind would rise in greater development and harmony, to qualify themselves for renewal of the ancient wisdom and knowledge. This is when the emissaries from both the evil and benevolent worlds and dimensions will come forth to reclaim man, either in honor or to draw him back down into deeper disgrace and ignorance.

At the beginning of each new age efforts are made to draw forth the purified man. We are presently 23 years into the New Golden Age, The Age Of Aquarius, and the so-called "Aliens of Light" are working very vigorously with those Earthlings who have made UTMOST efforts to align themselves in perfect rapport with the Cosmos and have released all reverse and rebellious concepts of life.

The farther away from our Sun a planet is, the greater degree of inharmony is present. The nearer, the more harmony. Therefore, it stands to reason that those from Venus on up are higher evolved and those from Mars on down have a lesser degree of order about them. The "Alien of Darkness" makes himself appealing only to the five senses and man's reverse values. The Alien of Light appeals to man's higher senses which are anchored upon virtue and all that establishes peace and good among the family of man.

There are aliens all around us. Many hold key positions, especially where technology is involved. The Aliens of Light are NEVER involved in anything war-related; that is an important clue. There are certain specific Earthly races that are actually alien to this world. Other races are wholly natives of this planet. The Chinese race originates from beyond Earth. Their former world was demolished through a vast explosion. A large space-fleet of them escaped and landed upon the moon's surface eons, ago when it was a lush-green sphere. They established their home upon it's exterior until it was bombarded, which forced the race to once again take flight in their "FIERY DRAGONS" to the Earth's surface.

The ancient Chinese legend of the sacred fiery dragon was derived from their antique cigar-shaped space ships that safely transported them to this planet's surface. I am uncertain of the history of the English race, except that they were exiled here. It is a fact that the English language is the most ancient of all tongues in the universe, contrary to the modern belief that Latin is the oldest.

There are other (hidden) Earthly races that originate from the Great Beyond, which dwell within the vast cavern-networks beneath our feet, as well as the great inner-hollow of Earth. There exists a gigantic race, a mile in height, imprisoned within the Earth's very central core. They are totally evil, possessing a form of dark immortality. Their former home was the invisible tenth planet, Planet X. They came here to conquer and did cause great strife and peril, for their main source of food was human flesh. They nearly annihilated mankind before a power greater than they was employed to capture and imprison them. They cannot be killed and it is hoped that a way will be found to reach their higher minds and begin to transmute their dark ways into good.

One particular breed which is of an evil alien origin are those of the SERPENT RACE. The escapades of that race in ancient history was the actual source of the legend of the serpent in the garden as recorded in the Holy Bible. They originally came to Earth to also enslave humanity and use us as a food source. They endeavored to rule the Earth and breed man for cattle. The Serpent Man was mighty in stature, between twelve to fifteen feet in height and powerful in influence over the weaker races. They were endowed with potent hypnotic powers to capture the cooperation and control of the masses. That hypnotic capacity enables them to project a false image of the person they choose to imitate. They select national leaders or positions wherein they have influence and can sway our minds; such as teachers, entertainers, writers, ministers and politicians. They cannot project their false image until they find a victim or body.

Occasionally they will kidnap a leader and later release them to serve their sinister purposes. The victim must pass through poor health, experience a serious accident, be kidnapped and unknowingly die, for them to take on the impersonation. If the person is knowingly dead, they may even "miraculously" resurrect to the inspiration of those religiously inclined. The Serpent can only occupy a body for a limited length of time, which varies with each individual. Eventually he forgets the original body semblance and the individual begins to take on drastic body and facial alterations. When that begins to occur, the Serpent must prepare to release that body. By the time that death takes place, the astral body is so dissolved that often the body will literally vanish.

There are three political leaders that I feel were and are of the Serpent Race. The first is Franklin D. Roosevelt; during his latter years in office. The reason I suspect he was, is that there arose cause to re-open his coffin. When it was, they were shocked to find it empty. The next person suspected was Hubert Humphrey. Please REALIZE that the original owner of the body was not necessarily of an evil consciousness at all. The leader's life then begins to channel off into peculiar directions often sympathizing with extremist's causes. The Serpent, under the leader's guise, finds appeal to those who are rebellious to society and government. Social misfits become their supporters and likewise their distorted channels through which to direct corruption.

Perhaps the reader may recall when it was publicized that Fidel Castro was murdered. A very clear, close-up photo was taken of his dead body which was widely published throughout the world. A couple of days later an apology was printed claiming an error: that his "double" was murdered instead. That, I am certain was a cover-up for a serpent take-over.

The Serpent's threat of dominion occurred about 50,000 years ago, beginning on the continent of Lemuria, which occupied nearly the entire Pacific Ocean. They overthrew that mighty culture, spreading their vile influence across continents to Atlantis. Through their corruption and threat to all planets, it was necessary to attempt their annihilation by causing the Earth's axis to shift. That change was accomplished in order to preserve humanity. Prepared places of refuge received the survivors prior to the shift. Most Serpents were destroyed, but a few endured. Because of their reptile form, they are cold blooded: freezing them will not harm their bodies. Earlier in this century a vast system of caverns were discovered beneath a glacier in Siberia, Russia.

Many humanoids were found frozen in perfect preservation along with a fleet of ancient flying saucers. The Russian scientists carried many frozen bodies to civilization. There, under carefully supervised and mechanized laboratory conditions, they were slowly and tediously thawed out. Some bodies proceeded to immediately decompose, while others amazingly displayed animate life and actually revived. Those of course, were the Serpent Race. Until that time Russian communism was no true threat to the world. Presently Russia is a very real menace. Communism, in the reigns of the Serpent, is like a violently wretched plague infesting the world into hopeless bondage.

Many UFO's we see are occupied by Serpents. Only they can navigate them, for the vessels are operated by MIND CONTROL. Man has not evolved his mind enough to pilot the antique saucers; even to think of crashing, would cause the ship to do so.

Some of the negative traits of the Aliens of Darkness is that they hypnotized witnesses or victims; they exercise force-tactics and protect their interests by instilling fear through threats and bodily harm. Frequently the Aliens of Darkness are either ugly or unpleasant to look at. Their eyes are often snakey or cat-like in appearance. They may emit unpleasant odors or offend any or all the five senses with their disorderly impression. There are many Aliens of Light that are entirely different than we, yet they express beauty to our senses. The Alien of Darkness may promise a contactee wealth, fame and power as a lure or reward for evil deeds. They will cause memory loss, resulting in ill health and horrible nightmares.

On the other hand, the Aliens of Light are here to preserve life, to restore balance and to extend wisdom, knowledge and the ancient secrets to all humanity. To help prepare man for the last great catastrophe, and then the restoration to a perfect Edenic world.

The last catastrophe is very near. Possibly within the next 15 years, or it may even occur much sooner; before 1985. The exact time is unknown. It may involve a devastating global war or vast earthquakes. Possibly a combination; quakes triggered by mighty nuclear bombs. The Aliens of Light are here to help those who will accept them.

The second Alien of Light that I know of and have made indirect contact with, is a starship commander from Venus. He was sent here to help guide the American people on the rough road ahead and then aid in building a new nation and world. He spent three years in the Pentagon under very close scrutiny. He openly revealed his identity and mission and met several times with the president and vice president, unveiling to them his purpose and assignment to America. Much of his mission was not permitted, such as greater healing and medicinal methods. He was highly suppressed to the acknowledgement of the general public. Because of the suppression, he befriended a man devoted to uplifting humanity through his teachings. In cooperation with his friend, the Venusian

Master, Valiant Thor, he has begun to achieve his original goals at a somewhat slower pace. Thor is an immortal. He continually presents a youthful appearance of a man about 24 years old. He is handsome, serene and very much a loner. One peculiar trait which perplexed the Pentagon was his absence of fingerprints. All perfect immortals have no fingerprints. Fingerprints are an omen of fallen irian, or mortality.

I believe within the next 15 years, Valiant Thor will be a familiar household name. Along with that, many great changes are and will continue to occur throughout the world in very rapid succession. Spiritual, mental, physical and environmental alterations are happening. Why? Because the Cosmic Ray is pouring in vastly stronger than it has for millions of years. What does that mean? It means metamorphosis; total and drastic species modification. Perhaps Earthman will grow another set of arms, or sprout ten fingers and ten toes on each hand and foot. Perhaps we will return to gigantism or regain the faculty to telepath. During the prehistoric ages evolution from sea to land was much more rapid than we realize. Most of it took place within the span of 100 years. Because the Cosmic Ray has once again increased it's flow, it is altogether possible for present Earth man to acquire the image of an uncommon alien or for an uncommon alien to adopt our present appearance.

Most aliens, regardless of virtue, choose not to be detected unless it is their preference. They can perform their mission with much greater ease and success if they remain undetected. When they are recognized, a well known human weakness takes grip and people overlook the message the visitor has to offer man; only to focus their consciousness on the phenomena and the messenger themselves. They place the subject upon a pedestal to make a God or Messiah out of him.

Present day man has hopefully evolved enough to avoid such a snare to sufficiently welcome the alien Messengers of Light for the purpose of their mission.

Alien space ships come in many forms. It is a known fact that those who navigate the cigar ships, the spheroid, and some of the saucer-shapes are of a peaceful order. One must be very cautious about all other forms. Among the most dangerous are those vessels that have angular forms.

There are certain saucer-shaped forms that are vehicles of the serpent race, retrieved from Siberia. Those vessels are frequently spy ships.

Often the Aliens of Light have the power to appear or disappear at will. As an example, about 15 years ago my parents lived in a remote mountain home, accessible to only by about 10 miles of dirt road. One peaceful summer evening as my father weeded his vegetable garden, he heard the crunch of gravel upon the road. Peering over his shoulder, he saw a good- looking man dressed in a suit with a briefcase, approaching. Slightly puzzled, he turned his back to continue the weeding process.

Presently he felt eyes watching him and swung around to find the young man standing nearby in observance. As he speechlessly gazed, the visitor proceeded to say only six words, "Remember 1982 and keep your faith." He then quickly retraced his steps back down the gravel road, leaving my father totally mystified. He looked away for only a few seconds, but when his gaze returned, the mystery man had vanished into thin air. Since then he has often pondered the meaning of the message.

Many people are aware that in 1982 the planets in our solar system will align in a very rare aspect. It is speculated that vast earthquakes will result, or possibly it will indicate the advent of some very trying events to besiege the world in relationship to civilization or culture. Certainly the alignment will indicate global change on a large scale, and certainly the Aliens of Light are aware of those coming changes.

That is why the Great Ancient Ones have given so much of themselves as helpers of humanity. We cannot weather the coming storm alone, we must have assistance from every possible superior being. Unless, however, we are reaching for and seeking to evolve ourselves into better beings, we stand little or no chance of rescue. Man must open his mind to new concepts, he must prepare himself to take the hand of the Alien of Light and walk forward into New Worlds.

"Behold, I make all things new." Rev. 21:5.

I have come to believe that some UFOs are occupied by what we can call demonic forces – though maybe I am drawn to this conclusion because of my own interest in horror. After all I am Mr. Creepo host of many horror flix. See www.mrcreepo.com

CHAPTER FOUR: EMISSARIES OF PEACE

THERE is sufficient evidence that at least some aliens visiting Earth have our well-being in mind. Donald Fender doesn't seem to be the type of person to make up a tall tale and that is why the Clarksville (Tenn.) *Leaf-Chronicle* of Feb. 2, 1977, probably decided to publish his account, no matter how incredible it might seem on the surface.

GREENVILLE FARMER CONTACTED BY BEINGS FROM OUTER SPACE?

Was it fact or fiction? Was it the fatigue of a travel-weary mind or a science fiction story come true complete with a visit from inter-galactic beings?

Whatever it was, Donald Fender believes it, enough to pay for a trip to Washington, D.C. to talk about it.

Fender, a Greenville, Tenn. farmer says he was "contacted" by beings from beyond the reaches of our planet while traveling on 1-40 Thursday, January 27.

Admitting, "It's unbelievable, people will think I'm a crank," Fender related a story of a visit from some interstellar travelers while he was driving along 1-40 on his way to Madisonville, Tenn.

Although many points of his story do not stand up to a critical examination, Fender contends he saw what he saw. He believes it to the point that he says he will spend his own money to travel to Washington to tell the authorities what he experienced.

THE AUTHENTIC BOOK OF ULTRA-TERRESTRIAL CONTACTS

According to his story, he was about 15 miles out of Clarksville on 1-40 headed toward Nashville when he felt "like someone wanted to talk to me." Surrendering to an urge, he turned off the interstate and traveled a side road to a point where he came upon the "spaceship". The ship resembled a pullet egg Fender said, and appeared to be a silky balloon or parachute. Fender said some beings came out of the vehicle, and spoke to him. They related a story right out of a Buck Rogers or Rod Sterling novel about being from a planet not visited by humans or their machines yet, Fender continued. They said they were here as emissaries of peace. These beings, real or imaginary, stated they had stopped where they did — and Fender can not say for sure where near Clarksville it was because it is the only place they can enter the Earth's atmosphere. Their mode of travel is restricted to a space vacuum that is aligned where the road runs north and south through Clarksville, Fender said they told him.

There are supposed to be two of these vacuums, one for the beings Fender talked to and one for another planet, Fender said. There is no way to cross over from the one on the east side of the road to the one on the west side of the road or visa-versa, he noted. These creatures supposedly create this vacuum, Fender said, and this first visit was apparently a type of test run.

"They said they were coming back," Fender noted, "They didn't say when, they just said they were coming back." The significance of the Clarksville visits, according to Fender, is that this will become the future home of space travel.

The visitors told Fender that because this is the only place where the time warp type of vacuum can be created it will become the place from which all space travel will originate.

Fender realizes his story is hard to believe, at best. "If anyone told me a story like this, I'd tell them it is a crock of baloney," he stated. He said he couldn't believe it himself, and decided against telling anyone until Monday morning when he called the Leaf-Chronicle with his bizarre story.

A bee farmer with a 253-acre bee farm, Fender is also a member in good standing with the Baptist Church in Greenville and a tobacco, corn, cattle and hog farmer, he said.

The sighting is said to have occurred at about 2:30 p.m. when Fender was headed towards Nashville on I-40. The whole experience took about 15 minutes, he said, although time seemed to stand still while it was happening. Fender also claims he was headed to Madisonville, Tenn. from Greenville, Tenn. to buy some farm equipment. Greenville is about 60 miles east of Knoxville and Madisonville is about 40 miles southwest of Knoxville.

Fender would not say what he was doing west of Nashville on a trip to Madisonville from Greenville, stating only that he had some private business to transact.

He also said he was in Madisonville at about 4:30 p.m. the day of his experience. Madisonville is more than 200 miles east-southeast of Nashville.

Air control officers at Ft. Campbell Airfield report no UFO sightings in the area on Jan.27, a Ft. Campbell spokesman said, although some floating lights were reported at Madisonville, Ky. Monday night. Those lights were from military helicopters on maneuvers in the area, the spokesman said Ft. Campbell had 87 aircraft in the Madisonville, KY., area Monday night.

Fender, 48, is not discouraged by any of these apparent contradictions to his story, however. He said he will pay for a trip to Washington to talk with whomever he is supposed to talk to there, and to find out just what "they want to do" about his sighting. "I've often thought if anything happened to me like what happened to those boys in Mississippi — who claimed to have been taken aboard an alien spaceship — I'd be ashamed to tell it, but I want to tell this," he said.

Back on June 7, 1977 the Atlanta (Ga.) Journal ran a story in which a man said UFO beings would be coming in 1982 to save mankind from destruction. This was long before such books as UFO Prophecy and my own Psychic and UFO Revelations. Maybe what Norman Chastin told columnist Ron Hudspeth is true.

Ever seen a UFO? Darrell Simmons, a Journal sports writer has. "I don't admit it though," laughs Simmons. It happened one night 16 years ago when Simmons and a college buddy were riding on U.S. 41 near Barnesville.

"There was a green flash in the sky," recalls Simmons. "I turned to my friend and said, "You didn't see that, did you?" He said 'No!' I said, 'Good, neither did I.'"

Admitting one has seen a flying saucer is equivalent to making room reservations at the cuckoo's nest. But Norman Chastain doesn't care. He's met a space creature. Even grew five accidentally in his backyard. He also expects to meet one again.

Chastain, a 67 year old retired railroad man lives out in Decatur.

Relax, DeKalb County residents, no little green men have been spotted in your neighborhoods lately. The experience that changed Chastain's life happened five years ago when he was living in Jacksonville, Fla.

One January morning before dawn, Chastain was fishing in the St John s River near the shore. Suddenly, he says, an object with brilliant orange and blue lights appeared over his boat.

At first, he thought it was a helicopter. "I'd never seen a flying saucer and I didn't believe in 'em", he says, "but then I made out the outline of it, and it was about 75 to 10 0 feet across and hovered about 100 feet over my boat." Just as suddenly it disappeared, says Chastain.

In the excitement his boat ran aground. He went down the beach to find a piece of timber to pry his boat out of the mud.

When he returned, Chastain's space creature was standing near the boat. "It was the most unbelievable thing you could imagine," he says. "It was gray, sorta of a color that reminded me of an old man's long winter underwear. It had black bands on its wrists, huge eyes, and open mouth, and the top of its head glowed like a big lightning bug."

Chastain says he stared at the creature for a moment and it peered back. "Then he reached down to a black box he had on his belt and there was a terrific white flash. The next thing I knew I was paralyzed. I couldn't move anything but my eyes."

Chastain says he lay on the beach until sunrise when the numbness finally left him and he was able to get up, climb into his boat and go home. "I was okay," he recalls, "except for this awful smell."

When he got home, he drained the seawater from his boat in his backyard. Yep, you guessed it. Three days later, a creature's head grew out of the ground...not one, but five.

"They were pink and shaped like human heads, but they resembled the creature even more," he recalls. "My wife said they were pink devils. I thought I was losing my mind."

Chastain took his story to the Jacksonville Journal and today proudly displays a newspaper clipping showing him holding one of the heads he had dug up with a shovel. It looks a lot like what Chastain described.

"After about three days they all shriveled up to nothing and died," says Chastain.

Deformed mushrooms? Not so, claims Chastain. "What would you do if you woke up and one of these were in your backyard?" he said, handing me a glossy photo of one of the heads. I assured him I wouldn't water it.

Since that experience, Chastain has become a UFO fanatic. In a shed in the backyard of his Decatur home, he'll proudly show you what he labels "The Most Outstanding UFO News Display on Earth." It contains maps, charts, newspaper clippings, tape recorders and even correspondence with "*Chariot of the Gods*" author Erich Von Daniken.

The 16-foot boat he used on the fateful trip sits near the shed. It has been renamed "The UFO."

He's made 30 trips in the last year to explore caves near LaFayette, Ga., where he's convinced space beings once visited. He's writing a book. Don't plan on reading it soon. It can't be completed until 1982. "What's going to happen will startle the world," he claims. He says space creatures from a distant galaxy will visit the earth around 1982 to save it from what he forecasts will be a giant earthquake that could kill a third of the earth's population.

"These aliens have controlled the earth's movements for millions of years," he says. "Their intentions are peaceful and they know all about us."

Next time you're at Stone Mountain keep your eyes peeled. Chastain says the mountain has been used as a navigational point by the space creatures for thousands of years and will be utilized again. "When they return, the Confederate Memorial will be the second tourist attraction at Stone Mountain," he says.

I had to agree with that, but couldn't help but wonder what they'd charge you to get into the park to see little green men.

"I'm down to earth," says Chastain. "I like fishing and a lot of other things. I'm not crazy and I'm no crackpot."

He thinks the CIA has covered up UFO sightings and proudly points to the fact that Jimmy Carter has admitted he once saw a UFO. "I hope he's going to reveal what has been kept secret," says Chastain.

Meanwhile, Norman Chastain has his eyes to the sky. "I'm waiting," he says. "I'm not going to make fun. They laughed at Columbus."

* * *

This next account is from a woman in Italy who sees the space aliens as being benevolent. After a life long relationship with the space beings, Germana Grosso breaks her silence and speaks out to the Turin newspaper.

SPACEMEN SEEK LOVE, NOT WAR

Beings from outer space have set up bases on earth beneath the Gobi Desert and even in Italy, according to a quiet 53-year-old spinster, Germana Grosso, who lives with her mother.

Miss Grosso said she has been in touch with them for 20 years and they told her: "Our main enemy on earth is the complete lack of mutual love and understanding amongst humans." She said she has been chosen by them to issue an urgent appeal "choose love, not war."

On July 10, spacemen told her "there will be an immense catastrophe for earthmen when a terrible earthquake will cause many victims." Shortly afterwards, China and the Philippines were struck by earthquakes.

On May 29, Miss Grosso was told "a volcano is going to erupt with tremendous violence." She is certain that this meant La Soufriere Volcano on the island of Guadaloupe.

Miss Grosso is respected by all her neighbors. She is calm and thoughtful and in no way hysterical or excitable. How did she start contacting spacemen, resulting in several thousand typed pages of telepathic messages from them?

"I started 20 years ago through a Tibetan Lama who contacted me by telepathy," she said. "He explained that I could converse with beings from outer space."

Soon she was speaking to them and seeing them as though on a television screen. She has painted over 70 surrealist pictures of spacemen with long ascetic faces, large eyes and long hair as well as female dragonflies floating about in an ethereal world.

There are also Egyptian scenes from the times of the Pharaohs all in microscopic detail.

Although Miss Grosso has no scientific education, many of her typed space messages contain highly technical terms. Miss Grosso said that these beings from outer space were named "Back" living on a planet called Lioaki.

They have numerous bases on earth already. Miss Grosso maintained, with one under the Gobi Desert and another under Sousa Valley, northern Italy. She said this base accounted for the number of flying saucers seen in this region in the past three years.

The "Back" spacemen also had a base deep under the Atlantic Ocean and this accounted for the series of mystery sea and air tragedies in the so-called "Bermuda Triangle" as ships and planes tangled with arriving or departing spaceships.

Miss Grosso said she had broken her 20-year-old silence at the urging of the spacemen to launch an urgent appeal for world brotherhood to save earth from a disaster.

The spacemen are only interested in giving a warning, and do not want to interfere with human history or earth's destiny, she added.

"Humanlike beings from other time continuums are here to assist mankind's development into the fourth dimension," says Mary Hardy, a Michigan housewife who has had a long involvement with space intelligence. She tells her story this way:

ALIENS ARE HERE TO HELP US!

"Since my husband and I built a specially designed pyramid we have been contacted by aliens (Space Brothers) from higher planes of consciousness. This is their explanation as to why they are here.

"They came to teach and to help humanity make the transition into the fourth dimension. This is necessary because the earth will be advancing into a higher electromagnetic frequency.

"In 1982 when the planets form a line in space a new progression of evolution will take place in the solar system. It will be the start of the birth of the planet Vulcan. For about fifteen years the solar system will be disrupted. At this time the earth will move its orbit to the fourth position from the sun. Earth people will find themselves entering the fourth dimension. Matter will not exist as we know it now. The vibratory rate or electromagnetic frequency will advance to what scientists call the fourth dimension.

"Our scientists are just beginning to understand this new knowledge. It will be called The New Science. Understand it is learning to use light at a faster speed or higher frequency. The atomic structure of light will be refocused into its sub-atomic particles. The sub-atomic energy level is called TACHYON ENERGY.

"The new science of controlling Tachyon Energy was formerly called Parapsychology or the supernatural control of mind over matter. When an individual deals with energy on its sub-atomic level - time and space are changed. Phenomena occurring by the use of Tachyon Energy will be greatly changed from the physical state that science now can test and study.

"Almost everyone has had a psychic experience. Most of these experiences occur on a sub-atomic level. ESP, Clairvoyance and the bending of nails and keys are all achieved by the person's ability to use sub-atomic energy.

"At the present time this energy is called Tachyon Energy because of its nature. Before you can ever have an electron, you have a mass of tachyons that wish to cohere together to provide enough energy to become all the other sub-atomic particles. Ultimately, they build up to form the nucleus of the atom. To "tach on" means to "stick to." Tachyon Energy is the glue of the universe.

"Energy in the atomic state (physical world) is nothing more than the slowed down Tachyon Energy. When light energy is slowed down the tachyons form the particles that make up the atomic structure of all matter.

"Our brains have the ability to function on atomic consciousness (physical) or tachyon consciousness (spiritual). The spiritual use of the brain can be achieved by going within as Jesus taught humanity.

"Science is on the threshold of understanding this. And with this understanding - time and space as we know it will change. Mankind will have entered the fourth dimension. The world will have given birth to the NEW SCIENCE.

"Jesus demonstrated the use of the new science when he walked the face of the earth. He said to each and everyone of us, "These and greater things you can do also." Jesus had the ability to change matter into its Tachyon Energy level and reconstruct out of the old, a new atomic structure. He did this by altering his mind energy. This is how he changed water into wine.

"The Hermetic student has always been taught the ability to use mind energy. The first step is to learn to see the electromagnetic energy field around all living things. When a person can see this he has begun to use the tachyon or third eye center in the brain. He has learned to see the light.

"The pyramid was given to mankind to help him develop this center. Pyr-a-mid means light in the middle. The pyramid refocuses light into a higher frequency so that mankind can learn to use and understand the fourth dimension.

"Jesus said, 'God is Light.' God has not hid himself from his creation. With the New Science the mind has been activated in such a way that the person can now use the Spiritual side of reality. He understands the Father's plan.

"The aliens are here to help us understand light. They are the messengers of the Father, the Light Bearers. History has known them as angels. They have existed throughout: all time and recorded history. When you can see the aura you can recognize the aliens or angels. There is a completed circle of light above their head.

"In this way they are known!"

I just came across this photo of John Keel and myself taken almost a decade ago in New York. The grand master of Fortean phenomenon was in good spirits as we talked about how St Nick might be an interdimensional spirit, king of the elfs. A master storyteller and good friend I can almost feel his spirit about.

CHAPTER FIVE: THE PRINCIPLES OF MOTIVE AND DESIRE

Before space aliens will communicate with you they must be certain of your motive and desire. They are not anxious for anyone to go out and make a "quick buck" off what they have to say. Nor do they wish to contact anyone who has only a frivolous interest in such matters. They are looking for people who understand their mission and can "get the word out". Though they will assist worthy individuals in times of great need, hey have repeatedly stated that their message is not just meant for a handful of men and women, but should be spread as far and wide as possible. Thus, when they do speak they will not usually talk on a personal level. What they want to get across is a lot more worldly in nature. Sometimes, they will help with personal matters if it involves spiritual development or a crisis that meets their requirements (centering normally around karmic influences). You shouldn't think of them in terms of having a few friends over to the house for tea. The Space Brothers have much to do and those who are assigned to help out on this planet must spread themselves "pretty thin" as it is. Thus, they take considerable care when it comes to speaking their mind. In order to "get through" to them you have to pass the test.

Through the spiritual messenger of Tuella (earth name Thelma Terrell, currently residing at the City of the Sun, a New Age community in New Mexico), we have been rewarded with a special dissertation on contacting the guardians who are trying to guide our development. This particular discourse was channeled through Tuella and comes from Andromeda Rex, Commander of a fleet of space ships circling the earth. His message will "clear the way" so to speak, so that you now will be able to approach the matter of attempting a space contact on your own.

A DISSERTATION ON CONTACTING THE GUARDIANS
BY COMMANDER ANDROMEDA REX

"There are five basic requirements which lead to successful communication between our dimensions, in conscious contact and telepathic thought exchange.

"First I would list QUALIFICATION OF MOTIVE. What is the motive in the desire? This should be carefully scrutinized and carefully searched by the participating soul. The desire must stand clean and undefiled by any self-centered purpose. The motive must be totally free of any desire for self aggrandizement or the flaunting of the self above others. The desire must be without any taint of launching a program that would return gain or fame to the souls so seeking. Wrong motivation will stop any seeker "in their tracks" toward advancement if it is born from an impure desire not in keeping with Light advancement upon the planet. Likewise, intellectual curiosity will bring no results whatever. Seeking in order to remove disbelief is another hindrance to results. One must believe in our presence before one seeks to converse with us. So let the heart be searched for perfect motive.

"Then, let DEDICATION BE THE INSPIRATION WHICH DIRECTS THE HEART IN OUR DIRECTION. The life and soul purpose of that one who desires our words must be one which has been dedicated to fellow men and the uplifting of the planet earth into its fourth dimensional expression and the fulfillment of the Aquarian Age on earth. For this we ever watch and monitor your world, seeking those hearts that are awakening to the greater picture, and the greater burden for a planet and its people. Those whose hearts bleed for the spiritual needs of humanity, and are dedicated to the coming of the Kingdom of God on earth, register our attention automatically.

"I am listing CONSECRATION as another basic requirement. This is an act of Love and Surrender of the human spirit to a Divine Purpose. Love is the strongest element in the Universe and the highest possible vibration upon your planet. It shines upon our monitoring board like diamonds across a dark sky. One who has begun to vibrate a life of Love to all Men, of all worlds, and is expressing that love to us in particular will in no way be ignored. That spoken Love will bring a like-minded response from our hearts to that one who seeks. For consecration added to dedication, builds a road or a frequency, along which our communications can travel back to the source of though which has been projected to us. Thus as you lift your loving thoughts higher to us and our octave, you enable us to return our own along that same energy path back unto you.

"Further, let me speak of CONCENTRATION. It is the nature of the human mind that it must be thinking of something, for it cannot be blank or motionless nor void. We therefore encourage concentration upon one certain thing, in order that mental activity in other directions can be erased. While one is thus concentrating upon one chosen thing, all else is shut out enabling one to subdue the busy conscious mind into stillness. Thus, if one will concentrate upon our ships in the higher atmospheres, thinking of our Love, our activities, and beaming Love to us in a quiet peaceful way, this action will be monitored and response will finally reach one who practices this discipline faithfully and regularly.

"I will close my thoughts on the matter by calling attention to MEDITATION. Now comes that moment of still waiting, that quietness within, like unto the quiet waters of a beautiful lake. Into this stillness, rigorously held intact by the mind, while in total physical and mental relaxation, will come the still small voice of heavenly response.

"Following these exercises one always gives thanks for that quiet moment spent with inner divinity, whatever its results may or may not have been."

Brad Steiger nicknamed me *Prince Of The City*. I guess I am a pretty wild character when the sun goes down. I've hung out with a few celebrities and talked UFOs with any number of rock and rollers like my long time friend Gaz of the Love Pirates.

CHAPTER SIX: TELEPATHIC CONTACT

HUNDREDS of UFOs at this very moment are said to be circling just outside the earth's upper atmosphere. The occupants of each craft have specific jobs—an individual purpose—for being positioned above our planet. Some are testing for radioactivity and other forms of pollution. Others are keeping a watchful eye out for interplanetary voyagers who, upon occasion, try to sneak down to earth for not so honorable reasons (such as to rob and loot our resources and possess human bodies for self-centered reasons). Still others are registering the vibrations of people to see how we are coming along spiritually. It is also claimed that they are trying to beam down helpful advice to those whose psychic centers are opened to them.

CHANTING

Jane Allyson of New York City, never concerned herself with UFOs before July 4, 1979. Along with two other individuals, Jane was standing on the roof of an apartment building on Bond Street in lower Manhattan waiting for the Fourth of July fireworks display to begin. "We were looking up-town in the direction of the East River, when we saw this brightly lit object set against a darkened sky." As the object moved closer, Jane and her companions could make out a definite shape — she said it was like a huge diamond star glowing in the sky. Jane says she was anxious for the craft to come closer so that all those involved could get a better look at this unworldly vehicle. Having had experience meditating, Jane began to lead those present in an American Indian chant. "With our eyes on the sky we began to chant Wo-U-Wo-Wo-Wo-Wo-Wo-Wo-U-Wo-

Wo-Wo-Wo-Wo-Wo-U. We continued with the chant for several minutes altering the pitch and holding it."

With each passing moment, the object kept moving closer and closer until, eventually, it got so near that the group thought the UFO was preparing to land on the roof where they were standing.

Jane admits that she was frightened and in awe at the very same time. "I felt drawn to this enormous craft, but also felt such a tremendous force that I realized, we could all be swept off the roof or crushed underneath the weight of the UFO."

Jane confesses that as they stood underneath the object "it seemed we might all break apart from the psychological pressure, until finally it disappeared." Later, inside one of her friend's apartments in the building below, Jane and the others became deeply moved. One of those who had witnessed this dramatic spectacle started to dance around the room as if hearing some inner music. The other person began to meditate for the very first time in his life. Meanwhile, Jane felt a tremendous state of compassion moving through her body, "producing such a powerful feeling of love for the entire human race, making me feel more alive than I had ever felt before." ;

Jane is convinced that whoever was aboard this "diamond" in the sky could mentally hear her and her companions chanting. "They recognized the fact that we were altering our consciousness; lifting our vibrations so that our bodies and minds were operating more in their dimension."

JANE ALLYSON

In a recent conversation, American Indian, Bleu Ocean, acknowledges that chanting has long been a means by which to communicate with the occupants of UFOs. "Our ancestors had special chants just for that purpose. They communicated with 'star people' on a regular basis and knew a lot more about the workings of the solar system than modern man is led to believe." Bleu adds that when contact was being attempted his forefathers were certain lot to wear anything made of metal. "They dressed simply and carried nothing ;hat might counteract the polarity of a hovering space ship. They knew that should they be wearing anything metal, that they might accidentally be pulled into the electrical field of the craft and suffer injuries."

MEDITATING ON AN INDIGO TRIANGLE

From what we have learned it is important to clear the mind of all mundane thoughts if one is to successfully contact our Space Brothers, meditating on a regular basis can speed up the process, and clear a path :o higher realms.

"Many of the members of a meditation group I once belonged to were m communication with extraterrestrial beings," notes Patricia Goff of Brooklyn, New York. Pat, whose background since childhood is that of an extremely gifted psychic, says the group had developed a viable means of talking to aliens who exist in other dimensions. "We would concentrate on a large painted indigo triangle. This triangle functioned as an open window into their world through which they can come and be with us, at Least for a brief while, in our state of consciousness." Pat explains that in this other dimension, the space beings see this indigo triangle as a golden beacon of light and know that someone wishes to speak with them.

Much to her astonishment, Pat says that at one of these meditations in alien actually crossed over and she could feel his presence in the room. 'The heavy metal mobile above our heads began to move around frantically and many of us could psychically sense an invisible force," she concedes.

RAISING THE VIBRATIONS AROUND YOU

One of the best areas to visit if you want to see UFOs and try and communicate with their occupants, is the rural town of Pine Bush in upstate New York. Hundreds of sightings have taken place here as well as a number of absolutely incredible close encounters. This community has been featured on PM Magazine, a nationally televised program as well as having been written up in *OMNI* magazine. Jane Allyson has driven to this area several times and has seen space ships more than once in the vicinity of Pine Bush. Jane says there is a reason why she is successful in "seeing things" here. "I try to prepare myself before attempting to contact them. In order for them to tune into your personal frequencies you have to raise the vibrations of the atmosphere around you. They can most easily pick up on a person who is at peace with himself and in a state of tranquility. It helps if you are psychic or if someone with you is gifted with sensitivity." Jane explains that as your consciousness is raised you emanate a bright light — a strong aura — which enables those operating in other frames of spatial reference to see us. "Some extraterrestrials cannot observe our physical bodies; they only recognize us by the light we give off."

FOLLOW YOUR INTUITION

Jane, as well as just about all the other contactees we have been in touch with, stress the point that it is necessary for a person to follow their intuition if they are ever going to succeed in becoming a legitimate channel for extraterrestrial intelligence.

"Many times you have to let an 'inner light' guide you" Ms. Allyson professes. "In the beginning the Space Brothers will usually try to communicate with you on a subconscious level to determine if you are ready for the more advanced course." Jane says that often they will come at night when you are sleeping. "Without realizing it most of us at one time or another travel out of the body. Once you are free of your physical form it is possible for them to> communicate with you very easily."

Jane also recommends trying automatic writing. "If your inner mind tells you to do it, sit down in a chair with a pen or at a typewriter and see what comes through. Automatic writing was one of my first attempts at contacting other intelligences."

If you have an obsession with the subject of UFOs or outer space in general don't try to suppress it. "If you get the urge to go out at night to a certain area, go there, don't stay at home. The Space People may just be sending you out in order to have a sighting. Often they will guide you to a place even though you may not initially realize what they have in mind."

MUSIC AND ART

Long before she was able to communicate with extraterrestrials, Jane says they began to have an important influence on her life. "Before I got involved in UFOs and psychic phenomenon I was writing songs and drawing. Suddenly, out of the blue, all my songs had spacey themes. I was writing tunes like Martian Love and The Visitor. One of the songs Jane wrote, Starlover, has been recorded and is played in Denmark.

Eventually, she would like to see an entire album made of this extraterrestrial music, which she feels is actually "inspired." One of the songs she is particularly fond of is *The Sky One Night*, which deals with an evacuation and earth changes, (the words of which follows):

Blue Violet Crimson Lights Glowing Swept Down Across the Sky One night.

And Over A Mountain A Second Sun. Spirits Were Chosen.

Then Those Born Blind, Those of Earth Will Remain.

Those of Fire Will Rise, And In The Center, All the Creators Were Turning Their Backs On The Educators. Pulled By The Moon In A Tidal Suicide.

Horizons Went Crazy And The Children Went Flying.

Colored Smoke Circles Pushing Away the Sky.

The Children Of The Earth Were Carried Into Space Tonight.

Star Streaked Spirals Jackknifed.

The Comets And The Landing Lights Glistened - And The Ships Uplifted.

Blue Violet Crimson Lights Glowing Swept Down Across The Sky One Night.

Among those who agree with Jane Allyson's findings are Lvnn and Anthony Volpe, New Age teachers from Pennsylvania, who communicate regularly with such messengers from the stars as Meeshandalek, an amphibian from the constellation of Pegasus, and Soltec from Centaurus.

"There are many ways for them to contacts," Lynn Volpe states. "Sometimes Space People ill send down messages modulated to your own brain frequency and thoughts will occur in your mind that haven't been there before. Many New Age inventions have been given to the world in this manner. Many people have thought of new songs and new ideas this way."

Lynn and Anthony relate the experience of a young man from their hometown who saw a UFO at five o'clock in the morning, just down the street from their residence. "He had just dropped his girlfriend off when he saw an oval-shaped craft traveling along side his car. He said there were orange lights all around it and fire spitting out the side. The youth blinked the headlights of his car off and on in an attempt to communicate with the UFO. The craft swooped down right over his car at this point barely missing it. It made a whirling sound as it passed and then went up to a hundred feet. By this time the young man had backed down in trying to communicate with the Space People because fear had replaced curiosity."

Today this same young man is an up-and-coming songwriter. "This space craft beamed down beautiful golden and violet rays of light and he was totally immobilized by it and couldn't move. He had been in a local rock and roll band, but now just about all he cares to write about are spaceships, brotherhood, UFOs and Space People."

The Volpe's believe that sometimes the Space People use golden shafts of light with messages coded into the light to record feelings and ideas onto our brain waves. "There are literally millions of space ships in the earth's atmosphere for different purposes," Anthony states matter of factly: "Some may be registering the vibrations of individuals while others are interested in upcoming earth changes."

Jane Allyson would be the first to acknowledge that UFOs have had a tremendous impact on her life. Shortly after her initial sightings Jane felt drawn to the area of healing. Today Jane is one of New York's accomplished psychic healers having lectured before doctors, nurses and psychotherapists at Bellevue Hospital. She has even progressed to the point of teaching classes in healing, where people learn how to heal themselves as well as others. Through her UFO contacts she has come to understand that her mission is to help this planet to evolve and become a more spiritual place to live.

CHAPTER SEVEN: "TALKING THEM UP"

ONE of the reasons it is said that the government keeps a tight lid on UFO matters is because they are afraid of mass panic. Most often referred to is the 1938 "War of the World's" radio broadcast in which the moderator, Orson Wells, told of a fictitious invasion of earth by Martians. Many of those who turned into the Mercury Theater late and did not hear the beginning of the program thought that warriors from the "red planet" actually were attacking — and killing — innocent people.

The Space People do not want anyone to panic! The truth is they only wish to communicate with those who have opened themselves up and are willing to serve as channels. They are not anxious to barge into anyone's home uninvited. They wish to arrive as welcomed friends. In the messages beamed down to earth by Ashtar, commander-in-chief of the Free Federation of Planets, we are told that in order to be receptive we should think of them in a positive light and be willing to communicate on a first name basis.

"It is important to think of us in positive terms. We will come to those who do. (If you wish contact) think of us as if you know for sure we are real". To spark a contact Ashtar recommends imagining "a giant ship surrounded by a blue glow." He also suggests that people "make drawings of us and our craft. Tell people to look at UFO pictures." Ashtar also strongly advises that those attempting to communicate not be afraid to call them by name. "Tell them to think of Ashtar. Tell them to think of Aura Raines. (These are the names of various space people that have been encountered). Tell them to concentrate deeply on us. We will answer many of those who call. Tell them to have their tape recorders turned on so that they may record our messages. Tell them to get the word out."

PHYSICAL FORM

Though a great deal of their messages come via mental telepathy to UFO contactees who are channeled into the proper wave lengths, from time to time as situations allow, they do appear in physical form upon our planet. This, I think, is very well demonstrated in the cases I provide in the chapter titled "They Roam The Earth." The experience of Oscar Magocsi in another chapter, "Inside the Saucers" pretty well illustrates what the space people are referring to when they say we should talk about them and "play them up". We shouldn't be shy when it comes to acknowledging their existence. In a sense it's time that all us UFO believers came "out of the closet" and let others know exactly what's going on. Oscar Magocsi had never believed in the existence of UFOs much less space people. That is until he had an encounter of his own just outside of Huntsville, Ontario, Canada. However, after this experience changed his life he began to seek out information, read books, attend lectures and ask questions. This open-minded attitude of a seeker of knowledge eventually lead to a face-to-face meeting with a space person by the name of "Quinten" and another alien named "Argus". If Oscar hadn't opened up his telepathic centers and indicated he was anxious to know as much as possible about UFOs and their occupants, he would still be peering up into the heavens looking for "lights in the sky," instead of talking on a personal level with our interplanetary friends.

Laura Mundo, from Dearborn Heights, Michigan, has been involved in UFO related work for many years. Back in the 1950's she established the Flying Saucer Information Center and sponsored a number of public events. She once organized a lecture for the late George Adamski (a world famous contactee who claimed to have met a long-haired Venusian named "Orthon"), and over 5,000 persons attended. A charming woman (though upon occasion she has been known to over react emotionally), Laura says she knows what it's like to meet a real space person and has developed her own method for "getting in good" with them.

Her method coincides with what the space people have themselves said in many different communications — talk about them freely.

"Talk up to everyone that the space people are coming to remove those people whom they can in their insulated spaceships, as our atmosphere gets more and more unbearable because of the accelerating sunspot activity. Then one day it may suddenly dawn on you that you are talking to a real space person as they begin to ask very profound questions about outer space that only someone who has been there would know. You will know by that time that you are not to ask them who they are or someone might turn on them, but with greater training now from them, you should continue on with your job, talking-up the space people's coming and the emergency to the planet, perhaps lecturing, writing or in some other way getting their message across."

If you "talk up" the subject long enough, Laura insists they will eventually get the message and they will come to you "behind the scenes, face-to-face, as they have to me. And then the two of you will go on, perhaps together now...to 'talk it up.' There is time for nothing else."

Like Adamski, Ms. Mundo professes to have conversed and met in the flesh "Orthon," a slender male Venusian with shoulder-length golden hair, and frail, but masculine features.

In 1958, Laura once again held a saucer convention and invited Adamski to speak as he had done years before. "Orthon, the man from Venus was there," Laura swears. "I was the only one to recognize him by his vibrations. He was a blue-eyed young man about five feet, ten inches, with a duck's tail haircut. He had beautiful white skin, although space people of all races are here. He nodded at me several times and smiled."

Almost two decades later, the same man looking exactly as he had in 1958, came to an event Laura was involved in. Laura was not feeling particularly well this day. It felt to her as if she were under "psychic attack, being drained of all energy. (As another person spoke into the microphone), I felt myself grow very sad, and sobs began to rise in my throat that I could not keep down." Laura maintains that she got the impression that something negative was trying to "possess me."

Laura left the stage actually screaming out in agonizing pain. "Suddenly this young man rushed directly from the audience to me. He held me in his embrace, repelling the negative power at once. He and my coworker led me to our booth and the curtained area behind it and put me on a couch. He worked on my neck until the pain entirely subsided. 'I don't know who you are, nor where you are from,' I told him, when I could once more speak, 'but I am very grateful to you.'"

Laura says the young man knelt down beside her, hugged her and proceeded to kiss her on the forehead. "He said 'God bless you,' and then left as quickly as he had come."

Laura's final words of advice: "Remember 'TALK IT UP,' LIKE WE HAVE DONE, IF YOU WANT TO BE 'TAKEN UP!'"

Keep the space people close to your heart and they will remember you. Think about them as you would your very best friends, because after all THEY ARE!

CHAPTER EIGHT: "STAR MAIDEN" FRANCIE STEIGER TELLS HOW TO CONTACT SPACE BEINGS

A shocking headline story titled "Invisible Aliens From Space Live Among Us," which appeared in the May 1, 1979, issue of the *National Enquirer*, has caused a great deal of controversy.

The story dealt with the fact that several top scientists with NASA and other governmental agencies now admit that beings from other realms, dimensions and planets are residing on earth having made themselves invisible under normal circumstances.

Francie Steiger's life-long ability to contact space beings who she maintains "exist among us in dimensions invisible to the average person," was recently evaluated by Forest L. Erickson, one of the nation's leading operators of the Psychological Stress Evaluator, a space-age lie detector. After an extensive series of tests, Erickson determined that Francie was telling the truth; that her verbal responses to specific questions did not allow for her to be lying or distorting the facts.

In an exclusive interview, Francie Steiger told *UFO REVIEW*, "There are many entities of varying descriptions who have been visiting and interacting with humankind for thousands of years. The most advanced of these space beings are concerned with mankind's spiritual advancement."

Amazingly enough, Francie Steiger insists that each one of us can learn the methods by which to contact these invisible space beings. "These beings have the ability to defy solid matter, coming and going instantaneously heeding not our laws of gravity as they enter our homes without means of a door. These beings are most commonly described as looking like angels. These are the intelligences with whom I am most familiar."

Francie reveals that, "Great historical figures, such as Socrates, Napoleon, George Washington, Joan of Arc, and Bernadette of Lourdes had contact with these beings. Some of mankind's most famous inventors, musicians, writers, poets, scientists, and political leaders have been visited by these beings. Our most influential thinkers and artists have been inspired to do their best work by these intelligences."

Contact with these entities is continuing she notes, "As before, the ministering beings wish to help all of humankind to enrich our lives with their wisdom, to make us more aware. Such contact is possible for all who sincerely follow techniques of communication, such as those which were given to me by the entities themselves."

Francie stated that in order to prepare oneself for contact it is very important to attempt conscientiously to erase hatred toward others. "Filling yourself with unconditional love is the all-important first step," she emphasized. "If properly done, you will actually begin to 'feel' an enveloping warmth surrounding your being."

Next, Francie suggests relaxing each part of the body, starting with the feet and moving upwards toward the face: "Rapidly tighten the muscles, then gradually relax them as you move upward. With your eyes open or closed, picture circles emanating from in front of you and slowly enlarging until they encircle your body. Tell your body that it is going to sleep, but tell your mind that it will stay awake and aware."

Francie says that there are many props which aid in relaxation, such as background music, flickering or revolving lights, and/or luminous stars that adhere to the ceiling.

"In the initial stages, it is very important to focus your conscious mind on an object for a period of time so that you can successfully separate the conscious from the subconscious and learn control of the latter," Francie states. "You must learn to put your physical body to sleep while awakening your spiritual self."

Francie went on to illustrate how one of her most interesting contacts with the space beings came by staring at a picture of a holy figure.

"I seated myself on the floor on a soft cushion. At lower than eye-level I placed a large picture of a holy figure for whom I felt great Love. I stared at the area between the eyes, not permitting normal blinking. As my eyes began to water and the room appeared to be darkening, I detected a small movement on the forehead of the figure. A tiny entity appeared and reckoned for me to follow." Francie felt that she was truly imagining him, yet she permitted herself to believe that he existed.

"I pretended that I was as small as he, and I followed him in my mind," Francie recalls. "I felt as though I were in two places at once. This realization began to 'break the spell' of the illusion, so I continued to pretend that I was small.

"Suddenly I found myself in outer space. The little man was no more, and I could see the universe clearly all around me. I felt as though I was suspended in space. I watched in awe as a vision began to spread out before me. I saw the incarnations of all humankind throughout the centuries until earth's fiery end. I became aware of a domain that I was told was occupied by the space beings and which was timeless.

"I was told of a plan whereby the beings had selected a group from among themselves to incarnate on earth and to live for a time to guide and to give us knowledge of the beyond."

On another occasion, Francie remembers seeing circles emanating from the wall opposite the foot of her bed, enlarging as they came toward her, encircling and moving upward over her entire body. A voice, more thought-form than sound, told her to picture someone of whom she was fond and to seat him mentally in a revolving-type chair and to cause him to spin. When she did this, she suddenly found herself spinning. A white screen appeared and she was hurled through it. She found herself on an unfamiliar mountainous countryside, watching a young boy tending sheep.

"I was then brought back to my bed," Francie says. "Twice more I was instructed to repeat this process of spinning my friend in the chair, finding myself projecting through the white screen, watching the same shepherd boy. It was then that I realized that this entity from an invisible realm had given me a new technique on how to project myself into other domains."

Francie maintains that with continued practice anyone may learn to establish an awareness of other dimensions. "Soon you will be able to thought-travel," she promises.

Thought-travel, she explains, is the means by which one will truly "each the dimension where space beings dwell.

In her consultation work with others, Francie has learned that some cross a bridge before they enter the domain of the space beings. Others speak of a golden temple wherein they are given special teachings. Many tell of a booming voice that inquires: "Are you ready?"

"If you hear that voice," Francie concludes, "say, 'yes' and you will make contact with the space beings just as I have done!"

CHAPTER NINE: SOLAR SPACE FOUNDATION

OF the many UFO contactees (there are probably more than 3500 all over the world), Robert Short of Joshua Tree, California, seems to be among the most persistent when it comes to channeling space messages on a regular basis. As director of the Solar Space Foundation, a nonprofit organization, the curly-haired Californian first discovered his ability to communicate with space people early in the 19 50's. In the beginning, the messages came through automatic writing and then more frequently as Bob sat in a chair allowing his mind to relax and be used as a receptacle for knowledge broadcast from thousands of miles away.

Over the years, literally, thousands of pages of transcripts have come through on almost every conceivable subject from world events to more personal matters. Once every week, Short sits in a circle with interested persons who come from all over the world to ask questions of his space alien friends.

On his methods for channeling, "each object in the universe emits various forms and levels of vibrations out into the atmosphere. Life forms tend to have vibrations that are more complex: especially those of humans. We are constantly emitting brainwave patterns such as alpha, beta, delta, gamma, and theta waves. In recent times, machines have been developed which are able to detect and record these brainwave activities. Each brainwave is happening at a different rate of speed of vibration, and represents various fields and intensities of activity. For instance, the alpha state is commonly radiated by a person who is meditating, watching a sunset or relaxing on a quiet beach, anything that slows a person down and increases receptivity. A pyramid is very useful in increasing alpha wave activity." Bob explains that "businessmen, stockbrokers, or a college student taking final exams are commonly thought of as being in the theta state."

According to Bob's philosophy, each and every action that we perform and also every series of activities, put out one or more of these vibrations. If the same activities are continually performed day in and day out, these patterns are sent forth into the universe and project our images through time and space."

Robert Short says that there is a computer on Jupiter that is continually picking up and recording all the brainwaves sent out by every man, woman and child on this and every planet in our solar system. These computer records are most commonly referred to as the akashic records, and not only do they have the records of each activity that we've performed in this life, but many past incarnations as well (on this and other planets throughout the universe).

By this means, the Space People are able to determine the purpose of an individual's present incarnation upon the planet, as well as probable future trends.

Short offers the following case history as a helpful example of the type of information that is stored on the computers on Jupiter.

"I have a friend in Lake Tahoe who had a channeling done for him. It was revealed that his first incarnation upon earth was as a cross between a cave woman and an astronaut in outer space from a UFO (similar to Bigfoot).

Since that time, he has incarnated upon earth some 250 times in various conditions. One of his incarnations was in the time of the Atlantean empire when he worked with sound and color to raise the vibrations of brain cells to increase awareness."

Short maintains that in the current evolutionary trends of mankind, it is important for us to rediscover the science of sound and color and how they relate to diet, the chakaras, environmental colors — all of which could enhance our life style. Bob says that as we approach the New Age of Enlightenment which many UFO contactees speak about, more and more people will have a greater and greater opportunity to rediscover what they were and what they are to be in the future.

One of those individuals who put his faith and trust in Robert Short is a young man who currently resides in Arizona. Charles Wren has lad a long time interest and fascination with UFOs and the arrival of aliens to earth. His particular interest lies in the area of channeling. Charlie tells about his first meeting with Bob in the following manner:

"I met Robert Short while I was in Lake Tahoe attending a conference organized by Lawrence Kennedy of Human Potential fame. Some of the topics discussed at the seminar included reincarnation, massage therapy, pyramid power, self hypnosis, tarot cards and UFOs. It was an all day event and I found much of what transpired to be of great use in my own personal spiritual development.

"One of the most unusual persons that I met at the conference was 3ob Short. He had a chart on the wall during his lecture which described low communications took place with a being on Jupiter he identifies as 'K'.

"Bob explained that 'K' wears a device called the resitronic translator which is much like our biofeedback machines, only much more sophisticated. There is a charged crystalline device placed at the top of this resitronic translator that can be tuned to the frequency of a person's) brainwaves just as a transistor radio can be tuned to a given radio frequency.

"Once 'K' has tuned in his translator, he begins to communicate with Robert Short by means of a relay system. 'K' sends his message to the mother ship which is located in deep space. The mother ship reads the message, OK's it for passage according to the laws of the space federation, it is then relayed to a small monitor ship in our atmosphere where it in - urn is relayed to Robert by means of a tensor beam."

Following the seminar held at the Human Potential Center, Charlie Wren attended a private workshop conducted by Bob Short in Lake Tahoe.

"The group consisted of a dozen individuals all of whom had come to ask questions of Bob's friends on Jupiter. Robert gave an introduction about his channeling and then went into a trance-like state. I was the third person in the circle and at Bob's request I had written down my question on a sheet of paper before the message session began. What came through from 'K' on Jupiter really blew my mind. The message had been poorly recorded and I was sort of hesitant about believing in all that was taking place. Suddenly, Robert looked at me and commented: 'That question requires information that we are not at present authorized to give. However, if you apply your talents and pursue this goal, then that which is asked about will be revealed to you in due time.' As far as I'm concerned, they had either read the information off my sheet of paper or had read my mind."

Charlie Wren says that a short time after his original reading he lent Robert five additional questions pertaining to his immediate plans. 'Even though Bob Short was in Joshua Tree and I was in Lake Tahoe a 400 mile distance), the computer on Jupiter was capable of finding me, reading my current brainwave activities and relaying the message to Robert y means of the tensor beam."

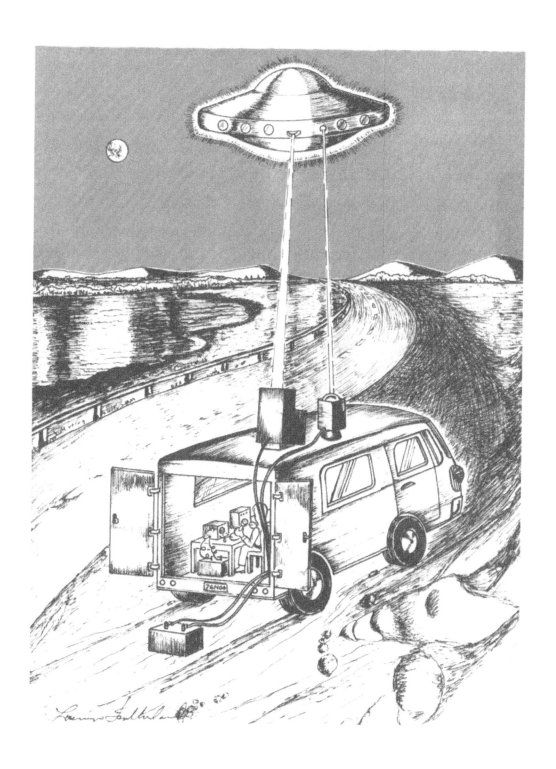

CHAPTER TEN: BEAMING UP

FROM our contacts with those who maintain close ties with the Space Brothers we have learned that though it helps to establish a psychic link with occupants of UFOs, even if one is not gifted with clairvoyance, it is still possible to communicate with them. While mind-to-mind contact may be the "ideal" approach to an unhindered friendship with extraterrestrials, actual equipment can be constructed at little cost to talk with them directly. In fact, an inexpensive light-beam communicator can be built for several hundred dollars which may be beneficial in contacting them on a one-to-one basis.

JOHN OTTO — A PIONEER

Though it is impossible to establish at this late date exactly who "invented" the first "light-beam communicator," researcher John Otto from Chicago (now deceased), first told of his interest in this form of electronic communication in the early 1950's. Said Otto: "Without claiming 'firsts' in any effort, for we find wherever we turn there is nothing new under the sun, it was nevertheless the sighting of a large cigar-shaped craft near Needles, California that spurred me into thinking of a radical new means of a communication attempt. Feeling rather stupid after shining a flashlight skyward while snuggled in a bedroll in the desert that night, the idea of light-beam communication was born for interplanetary spacecraft use. "

Economical to use and relatively simple in design, Otto's first light-beam communicator was a microphone into which he could speak. The communicator was attached to a power pack and a bright searchlight. A converter turned his voice into vibrating shafts of light which could be picked up on board a spaceship.'

One of those who knew Otto in the early days and went along with him into the desert several times in an attempt to contact UFOs seen quite frequently in the area, says that one night success came shortly after midnight.

"This giant craft appeared directly overhead and Otto started talking into his device. The beam from the light-beam communicator struck the metal hull of the space ship and the air was filled with a slight humming noise as the UFO seemed to acknowledge our presence. The ship tilted slightly back and forth as if whoever was inside, was attempting to respond. In those days Otto had not perfected a receiver to pick up messages from flying saucers, but later on I understand that he did."

A man with a good sense of humor, the robust John Otto liked to tell this rather funny story involving a friend of his who had been going outdoors on a regular basis with a light-beam communicator he had built using schematic diagrams drawn up by Otto. "He was continuously modulating canned music and sending out a jumbled jargon of words, always closing with 'How is my readability?' After several weeks he had a reception of the same type of material, jumbled, unintelligible words, and then some music. Finally came, 'How is my readability? Go ahead...' My friend did not have anything of importance ready to converse with his unseen communicator, so it floored him somewhat. This is why you should consider in advance any plans to transmit."

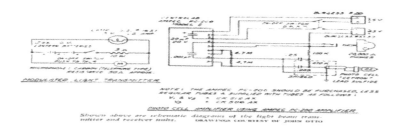

Shown above are schematic diagrams of the light beam transmitter and receiver units. DRAWINGS COURTESY OF JOHN OTTO.

AN UNUSUAL OCCURRENCE

Perhaps Otto didn't realize it — he never made a statement one way or another on the possibility — but in all likelihood, the space beings he was in contact with were probably responsible for transmitting telepathically the plans for the light-beam communicator he eventually came to get a patent on. According to Pam Miller and Ivan Ortiz, who have been involved in metaphysics, UFO research and spiritual development for over thirty years, many "New Age" inventions have been psychically beamed to earth by our Space Brothers, usually without anyone ever catching on.

At a recent conference in New York, the couple told this rather unusual tale: "A friend of ours who lived in the mid-west in the mid-1950's was receiving radio communications from space intelligences. This was all going along rather well when one day he went out to his mailbox and found a large envelope without a return address. He opened it and was rather surprised to find that it contained a set of plans to build a light-beam communications device. Since he was an electronics technician he went ahead and built it and used it and actually made contact." The man, according to Pam Miller and Ivan Ortiz, later joined a contact circle and shared his unusual finding with others.

STORY OF THE MITCHELL SISTERS

In at least one instance that we know of, plans for a communication device were given to those involved in a face-to-face meeting.

In the late fifties, two young sisters — Helen and Betty Mitchell - came onto the saucer scene very briefly with a most unusual story, involving a physical confrontation with aliens in a downtown St. Louis coffee shop. During this meeting, and several others that took place over a period of months, Helen and Betty were given the knowledge of how to go about contacting their space friends any time they wished.

"We had been shopping and had stopped off to get a coke and refresh ourselves," stated Helen Mitchell later on, deciding only to tell of her experience to a select, "open minded" few.

"While in the coffee shop we were approached in a very mannerly way by two gentlemen dressed in grey suits, who managed to interrupt into our private conversation. As they spoke to us we found that they were from a huge mother-craft orbiting the planet Earth, and that their names were Elen and Zelas. They told us that we had been very closely watched by the Space People for the last eight years, and that our progress had been noted off and on from the time of our birth. Betty and I were both inclined to think that someone was playing a silly joke on us and we laughed when they told us this, but they were not laughing and were serious and stern. We were strangely shocked, however, when they told us of a few incidents in our childhood that no one could have possibly known excepting the family.

"They told us that we had been selected as contacts by the people of space to serve as channels through which they could give certain information to Earth, and that we had been carefully watched, as I stated before. They told us of the reasons why the space people were coming to Earth and that they were here to guide Earth along the lines of Brotherhood and Science. We were very much amazed at their words, and we noted particularly the kindness and warmth that shone in their eyes. With a single glance from them we seemed to sense the vast wisdom and brotherhood which they must have lived among. After talking with us for a little over two hours they left and told us they would contact us again, but it was not until a week later that we were impelled to again return to the same coffee shop.

"When we entered the door we again saw one of the Space Brothers, and he gave us instructions at that time for building a device whereby we could contact the Space People. His instructions were explicit and precise, for he warned us that unless we placed every piece of the device in the proper place we would not be able to contact them with it. We were not allowed to take the drawn diagram of the device with us, but we had to remember it as it was explained to us. When we obtained the proper pieces for the device we constructed it when we returned home, and were happy to find the results were satisfactory. We were amazed when we tuned in on the mother craft and spoke with the same person we had earlier seen. We were also allowed to speak with the commander of the craft, who at that time was known as Alna. In the following six months we spoke many times with the Space People through the device, and received much information about their homes, sciences and craft."

Shortly after the sisters had their first contact, Helen was alone in downtown St. Louis on business when she was once again contacted by the Space People. At their request she drove with them to a heavily wooded area where she maintains she actually boarded one of their scout craft. She was flown to a large mother ship where she was taken on a tour.

"In one room I was shown the control section where I was told our calls were received when we operated our device. Here they placed a call through to our telephone in St. Louis by adjusting a series of dials, and I was allowed to speak with Betty and tell her that I was with the Brothers. I was also shown a scope similar to a television screen, the only difference being this was at a slight elevation on the control counter, instead of standing up at eye level or in a box-type cabinet which our television sets consist of. This scope could obviously reflect any particular building or house that the Space People desired to observe, and when I looked at the scope when Alna requested me to do so, I could see the inside areas of my home and could see my sister, mother and the children moving about. It was as though the entire roof had been removed and only the walls remained of the house. When I asked them how this was done, they explained that the first set of vibrations that left the roof were erased and the vibrations of the furniture and people inside were received on the scope, and therefore it appeared as though the instruments in the control section were actually looking through the building."

Helen and Betty Mitchell had many more contacts, but they soon faded from sight, deciding in the long run to keep their experiences bottled up inside because of possible fear of ridicule. Their whereabouts are unknown today.

BUILDING YOUR OWN COMMUNICATOR

Space ships have been landing on a regular basis on the property of the Solar Light Center located near a mountain vortex some 20 miles north of Medford in southern Oregon. The head of this New Age organization (whose purpose is to give forth educational, philosophical, and scientific teachings from advanced Space People), Marianne Francis, claims to communicate with the "brothers and sisters of light" who come in craft of shining silver to bring to earthman an extension of consciousness into other dimensions and spheres. "Their forms are humanoid, their communications are valid and their reality is incontrovertible," Marianne avers.

A representative of the Solar Light Center, K.M. Kellar, B.A., has released a set of plans for a simple light-beam communicator that anyone with a knowledge of electronics should be able to build without a great deal of trouble. Kellar describes this device in the following way: "Simple equipment for demonstrating the transmission of speech or music over a light-beam can easily be set up... for communication over great distances, more elaborate equipment is required. Such experiments show that there is no limit to the distance over which this equipment can be used. In fact as far as light will travel so will sound. Catching a properly equipped UFO in the line of these beams may be difficult, but experiments indicate that successful contacts have been made in this fashion."

K.M. Kellar testifies that once you have caught a properly equipped UFO in your sights transmitting a message is not that difficult as long as you have the right equipment. The Solar Light Center representative says building a communicator is not a difficult task, especially for someone with any training at all in electronics: "A simple transmitter for light-beam demonstrations can be made by coupling a public address system to a suitable neon bulb equipped with a parabolic reflector to focus the light into a narrow beam. Sound waves are converted by the microphone into electrical impulses which correspond in amplitude and frequency to the original sound. These impulses are amplified sufficiently to operate the neon bulb so that it emits light into proportion to the amplitude of each pulse. A direct current bias voltage is also applied to the neon bulb and adjusted to give optimum linear characteristics to the modulated light-beam produced by the neon bulb. This beam is focused by the parabolic reflector into the optical system of the light-beam receiver."

Below, we have demonstrated just how easy a device as described above can be constructed. Anyone with knowledge of electronics should have little trouble building such a device. Apparently, from what we have been able to learn, the Space People want those who are on their "wave length" to speak with them, and have readily given the plans to technically advanced equipment of this type to be shared with all of mankind. It's a crying shame that so little research has been done in this direction!

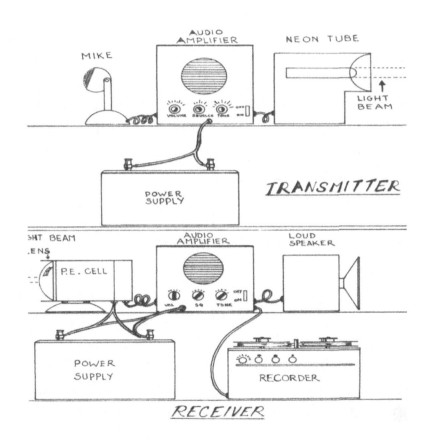

THE TESLA SCOPE FOR SPACE COMMUNICATION

Many years ago, long before the days when to many of us, the idea of communication with other planets was strictly a Buck Rogers fantasy, Nikola Tesla was already conducting serious experiments and inventing devices for communication with intelligent life on other planets. Furthermore, he was the first man in Earth's history to record receiving what he firmly believed to be intelligently controlled signals from outer space. Nikola Tesla was a genius born far ahead of his time, and while virtually unknown today he is the man who discovered the principle of alternating current. In addition, he held almost a thousand patents but refused to accept millions of dollars in royalties because he felt this information was being channeled to him and that it belonged to all of mankind and was not the property of any one individual.

Years after his contact with another world, Tesla revealed the circumstances under which contact was established: "In the year 1899, Nikola Tesla, with the aid of his financial backer, millionaire J.P. Morgan, set up at Colorado Springs, an experimental laboratory containing high voltage radio transmission equipment, a 200-ft. tower for transmission and reception of radio waves and the best receiving equipment available at that time. One night, when he was alone in the laboratory, he observed What he cautiously referred to as 'electrical actions which definitely appeared to be signals.' The changes were taking place periodically and with such a clear suggestion of number and order that they could not be traced to any cause then known to him.

In a written report, Tesla stated, 'I was familiar, of course, with such electrical disturbances as are produced by the sun, the Aurora Borealis and earth currents, and I am as sure as I can be of any fact, that these 'variations' were due to none of these causes. It was some time afterward, however, that the thought flashed upon me that the disturbances might be due to intelligent control. The feeling is growing constantly upon me that I had been the first to hear the greeting of one planet to another. Faint and uncertain as these signals were, they have given me a deep conviction and foreknowledge that ere long all human beings on this globe will turn their eyes to the firmament above the feelings of reverence, thrilled by the glad news Brethren! We have had a message from another world, unknown and remote!'"

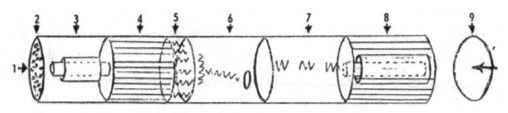

"Q" Glass Vacuum Tube enclosed in wooden box
9 ft. long, 5" in diameter

Legend:
(1) Audio Output. (2) Pick up. (3) Converter. (4) Automatic Control Chamber.
(5) Gas Chamber. (6) Converter. (7) Received Energy Control. (8) Dark Room (this
section enclosed in pure silver shield). (9) Head.

The above illustration has been copied from a rough sketch (not to scale) drawn by Arthur H. Matthews of the basic concept pf the design for a Space Communication Set which would increase the speed of electrical waves to 27 times that of light, as first conceived by Nikola Tesla in 1898, with the objective of communicating with the planet Venus. Due to pressures of other work, however, the first working model was not built by Tesla until 1918. In 1938, Arthur H. Matthews, under Tesla's guidance, built an improved version of this device at Sanford, in the Province of Quebec, Canada. In 1947, 3 years after Tesla's death, he rebuilt the set, incorporating further improvements and finally, in 1967, he reconstructed the Tesla Scope, adapting the new microminiature electronics and reducing its size to 6 ft. long and 4" in diameter. While the more recent models have incorporated the refinements of modern technology, this Space Communication Set retains the same basic concept as originally devised by Nikola Tesla and by this means, Mr. Matthews has, over the years, received messages from Space People who claim that they are from Venus.

Mr. Matthews states that the following message (abbreviated here because of space limitations) has been transmitted through various channels to the people of earth for many years and is the same message that he received via the Tesla Scope in 1941, 1947, 1949, 1951, 1957, 1959 and 1961. When first received, Matthews was told that the information came from Space People claiming to be from Venus and who traveled to earth aboard a spacecraft they called the X-12, a mother ship 700 feet in diameter and 300 feet in height.

"When you first receive this message, you will, like most Earth people, doubt. This is one of the strange things we find about the people of Earth - their continued doubting. They say they believe in God, but they doubt. They say God can cure their sicknesses and their troubles, but they doubt. Therefore, we expect you to doubt also. You will wonder if we really come from Venus - do we come from outer space? And you will wonder how we are able to talk to you in your own language. We use English at this time because you, our friend Matthews, only understand this language, but we have made a study of every language used by mankind. Actually, we would prefer to transmit our thoughts by the use of mental waves which would activate the Tesla machine.

"As we look down on Earth, we note the greatest confusion and misunderstanding. Instead of acknowledging the One God and looking towards Him for enlightenment, we find you all over the Earth running hopelessly and helplessly in pursuit of many things you think will increase your personal happiness - and yet you wonder why you continue to suffer. We hear all of you, year after year, asking the same questions: 'Why must we suffer? Why do we still have wars, sickness, poverty, famine and death? Why does pure joy always run away faster than we can, so that we can never catch up with it?'"

"The answers to these questions are to be found in the fact that instead of turning upwards to God, your thoughts are earthbound and you judge only by what you see in others around you, the vast majority of whom are sick, unhappy and full of bad habits, doubting the existence of the Supreme Being and futilely, you follow the group.

"Your Earth is full of hate and misery and this condition has come to be accepted as the rule for mankind on Earth. This is not how God intended life to be on your beautiful planet, but very few of you obey the Laws of God. Many of you attend some form of religious service on your Sundays, but how many Earth people carry out God's Laws in their everyday lives? We are amazed and saddened to find how much of your time is devoted to inventing and using destructive machines with which you murder each other. We see you spending vast sums of money pretending to bring peace on Earth, when you should know that the only way of obtaining peace is FREE - through Christ Love - there is no other way, so why waste your money and energy? We ask this question realizing that most Earth people have known for almost 2,000 years that the only way to secure peace on Earth and goodwill towards your fellow-men is by following the teachings of Jesus Christ whom a God of Love sent to your planet to bring spiritual enlightenment to mankind.

"Therefore, we can only sadly conclude that the Earth people must be suffering from some form of mental sickness which can only be cured in one way-the way of the Christ Philosophy of Love. You have heard all this before and much of what we say will fall on deaf ears, but our thoughts are directed to those few of the Earth people who have sufficient mental and spiritual power to think clearly and to know right from wrong. These few have been implanted among you to help others to evolve spiritually and to grow in a manner to be of service to the Great, All-Knowing, All- Loving God and all His creatures. Your present behavior is the reason for the continued visits to Earth by those of the Space People who endeavor to act as spiritual guardians to your planet, but we must warn you that if you continue to conduct your lives by wrong thinking, you will surely annihilate yourselves - and we shall not have many people to pick up when your Earth is about to be destroyed.

"To help the people of Earth, we brought down one of our own to live among you. During a trip from our planet to Earth, a Venusian child was born. We landed our spacecraft at midnight on July 9, 1856 and decided to leave this boy-child in the care of a good man and his wife. This infant was Nikola Tesla and we left him on Earth in the hope that his higher mental power and inventive genius would enable him to build advanced machines for the benefit of humanity and that your world, torn by hate and wars, would thereby come out of the darkness into the light. During the years between 1856 and 1943, we landed many times on earth, but we found no improvement there. At the death of Tesla in 1943, we landed again and attended his funeral. We were saddened to find that the Earth people had used the gifts of Tesla and other great inventors only to satisfy their greed and lust for power, that the same evil conditions existed on Earth and that its people continued to expend their energy on wars and killing their own kind, which is contrary to God's Law which clearly states: Thou shalt not kill.

"These things are beyond our understanding, for Venus, in all its history, has never had war. We have but one purpose in life - to serve God and this we do with all our energy of body and mind and because we do this our mental power grows stronger with age. We remain in perfect health until the day we die. We enjoy perfect harmony, health and happiness with our loved ones all the days of our lives. We have no place in our hearts for selfish desires because we know and believe that God's Law is good and therefore we have no need for man-made laws.

"Lack of faith in God has left your Earth in the Dark Ages and you will never progress or know peace of mind, true happiness and complete harmony until you learn to renew your faith and to become higher in your thinking and living than the crawling things which you now appear to emulate - instead of becoming spiritually-minded beings in the likeness of God. To avert hatred and wars, you must learn to remove every trace of national pride and racial discrimination, for there is, in fact, only one race in the entire universe - that of mankind whom God created."

Much research is needed in the area of constructing and utilizing such devices as the light-beam communicator and the Tesla Scope. Currently, I know of no scientist who is working with such equipment, once again proving that they have no interest in actually communicating with intelligent life in the universe. For the most part, they seem mainly interested in making money and prolonging the inevitable.

At Russian Base, Fidel Castro Was Shown a Captured Alien Spacecraft and the Corpse of its Pilot
By Jorge Martín

IN March 29, 2012 former President of Cuba, Fidel Castro issued another one of his written "Reflections', entitled "The need to enrich our knowledge."

In the letter, he discussed several issues related to the dangers for the survival of humankind posed by the current warmongering race that some of the world powers are enforcing, and how the bearers of these actions tend to be characters who suffer from a lack of culture and/or knowledge.

Given the above, he said a key factor in achieving a high degree of awareness is to obtain the highest possible degree of enrichment of our knowledge.

He discussed some of the current geo-political problems, but suddenly interjected into another subject, the possibility of extraterrestrial life in the universe around us.

About it he said: "When Pope John Paul II visited the country (Cuba) in 1998, more than once before his arrival I talked about various issues with some of his helpers.

"I particularly remember the time when we sat down to dinner in a small room of the Palace of the Revolution with Joaquín Navarro Valls, spokesman of the Pope, sitting across from me. To the right was a kind and intelligent priest that came with the Speaker and accompanied John Paul II at the Masses.

"Curious about the details, I asked Navarro Valls 'Do you think that the immense sky with millions of stars was made for the delight of the inhabitants of the Earth when we deign to look up some nights?' 'Absolutely'- he said. It is the only inhabited planet in the Universe '.

"I turned then to the priest and said, 'What do you think of that father?' He responded:" I think there is a 99.9 percent chance that there is intelligent life on other planets '.

"The answer does not violate any religious principle. Multiplied mentally, who knows how many times the figure, it was the kind of answer I would consider correct.

"After that, that noble priest was always friendly to our country. To share friendship you do not have to share the beliefs.

"Today Thursday, as occurs with increasing frequency, an European entity with knowledge published an article on the subject which reads, verbatim: "There could be thousands of millions of planets not much larger than Earth orbiting faint stars in our galaxy, according to an international team of astronomers.

"The estimated number of 'super-Earths"-planets with up to ten times the mass of the Earth is based on discoveries already made and then extrapolated to include the population of so-called' dwarf stars' of the Milky Way.

"Our new observations show that about 40% of red dwarf stars have a 'super-Earth" orbiting in their habitable zone, in which there may be liquid water on the surface of the planet", said Xabier Bonfills, head of the team of Sciences of the Universe Observatory of Grenoble, France.

"Because red dwarfs are so common, there are about 160,000 million of them in the Milky Way, this leads to the surprising results that there are tens of million of these planets in our galaxy alone."

"His studies suggest that there are 'super-Earths' in habitable zones in 41% of cases, ranging from 28 to 95%.

"40% of red dwarf stars have a 'super-Earth" orbiting in the habitable zone, where water can exist in liquid form. "

"That leads to the obvious question as to whether any of these planets is not only habitable, but has life."

"But these stars are given to stellar flares, which can bathe nearby planets with X rays or ultraviolet radiation, which may make less likely the existence of life.

"We have now to find traces of life on those planets," said The researcher from the Observatory of Genoa, Stephane Udry.

"If we can see traces of elements related to life such as oxygen in that light, then we could obtain evidence on whether there is life on the planet. '"

"A plain reading of these reports demonstrates the possibility and necessity to enhance our knowledge, enrich it, knowledge now fragmented and dispersed.

"We may take positions critical of the superficiality with which we address both cultural and material problems. I do not doubt our world is changing much more rapidly than we can imagine."

That much is written by Castro in his reflection, but what he discussed in it opened to us a door to reveal an important information we had known for some time, which due to personal considerations we had not published, until now.

In year 2002, the renowned Cuban filmmaker Octavio Cortázar visited Puerto Rico in order to participate in the San Juan Cinemafest (International Film Festival).

Knowing our journalisic expertise in the field of UFO research in Puerto Rico, he called us at the editorial offices of our magazine *ENIGMAS del Milenio*, asking to meet with us.

We met and he gave us a copy of the first documentary ever made in Cuba about the UFO topic, of which he had been co-producer.

The documentary, entitled "UFOs in Cuba" is an excellent production that seriously and responsibly reports the very interesting UFO incidence of the island of Cuba.

Cortázar was Vice President of the prestigious UNEAC (the Union of Writers and Artists of Cuba), and founder of the International School of Film and Television of Cuba, due to this, he was very respected in his professional field, both in Cuba and abroad.

During our conversation we exchanged information on UFO cases from our respective countries, Cuba and Puerto Rico, and he revealed to us something very important that had come to his knowledge due to his position of trust as vice director of the UNEAC.

He said that besides Fidel Castro meeting with the Speaker of the Vatican and other aides he had also discussed the issue of extraterrestrial life with Pope John Paul II himself when he visited Cuba in 1998.

According to Cortázar, Castro asked John Paul II what he thought about the possibility that man was not alone in the universe, and the Pope would have said that the probability of life beyond Earth was a fact.

They also discussed a wide range of data, even related to the observations of so-called Unidentified Flying Objects or UFOs.

We conducted a recorded interview with Cortázar and played the recording in our radio show 'UFO Evidence', on radio station NotiUno, excluding the details related to the meeting between John Paul II and Fidel Castro and their talk about extraterrestrial life, as Cortázar said he preferred it to be Castro himself who eventually revealed the fact.

We agreed not to publish anything about it until the right time to do it arrived, and now, with what was said by Castro in his reflection, we feel free to do so.

But what is it that provokes Castro's interest in the subject of extraterrestrial life?

Another information offered to us later, which came to from sources we consider irrefutable, gave us the answer to that question.

Castro Saw an Alien Spaceship and the Corpse of its Pilot

Later, during the celebration of the Puerto Rico Books Fair in San Juan, we presented our book *'Vieques: Caribbean UFO Cover-Up of the Third Kind'*, which deals on an apparent UFO/alien secret program the US NAVY had been involved with in the island-municipality of Vieques, which is part of the Puerto Rican archipelago.

Among other authors who were presenting their books at the fair was Attorney Juan Mari Brás, a well-known pro Puerto Rico independence leader and socialist, accompanied by Mrs. Providencia (Pupa) Trabal, another well-known and highly respected pro independence leader, who was very close to him and his family.

While talking with her about the content of our book, she revealed a series of UFO/alien experiences that she and her family had had, and suddenly she said, "You know something? Juan Mari Brás has important information about this matter that was given to him by Fidel Castro. "

Listening that struck us. Fidel Castro talked to attorney Mari Brás about the UFO matter?

Cuban authorities have always been very frugal at official level about the UFO situation, and to hear that Fidel Castro had personally given Juan Mari Brás information on the matter demanded us knowing more about it.

What did Castro say to Mari Brás?, I asked Mrs. Trabal.

"Well," she said, "on one occasion we were talking and the UFO subject came up, I do not recall why, and Juan, though many do not know it, was very interested in the subject, and told us that during one of the meetings he had had in Cuba with Fidel Castro, Fidel had told him something important.

"He said that years before the fall of the Soviet Union, Fidel had traveled to Russia and the Soviet authorities had taken him to a military base in which there was a special laboratory, and they showed him there a UFO, a spaceship, a disk they had captured, and the body of a tall extraterrestrial being, that they kept preserved in a special box-like machine (a cryogenic freezer?)."

'This is very important. It is the first time this information is known', we told the lady.

"I'm aware of that," she said, "and Juan had not spoken before about this, I think that because he thought Castro had told him this in confidence. But the fact is that he told us about it. And we believed Juan, because he is a person of great integrity, and would not say something like this if it was not true, and mostly if it had to do with Fidel Castro, who was his personal friend and for whom he felt great respect.

"I remember that he also told us that the Russians told Castro that they knew the Americans had a similar lab, a research center, with crafts and alien bodies," said Mrs. Trabal finally.

Later, we talked with Atty. Juan Mari Brás and asked him about what the Russians had revealed to Fidel Castro during his visit to the Soviet Union pertaining to the extraterrestrial spacecraft and the corpse of its pilot at the military base, and although he implied it was true, he would not elaborate more on the matter.

Today, with the statements made by Castro in his 'Reflection,' we are publishing this information as an exclusive revelation.

Plasetsk or Kapushtin Yar?

One question remains; which one was the military base Fidel Castro was taken to by the Soviet authorities, where he saw both the spaceship and the alien's corpse?

Recent reports have arisen independently talking about Area 51 type facilities in Russia, secret research similar to the one allegedly existing in Nevada, USA, where the USA Government allegedly keeps several alien spacecrafts recovered and/or captured, that are being studied to copy their advanced technology, as well as preserved alien corpses in special freezer-containers, for the purpose of examination, among other things.

One of the alleged Russian centers of this kind would be located in the Plasetsk Missile Testing Ground, located in northern Russia, which, 'coincidentally' for many years has been subjected to persistent surveillance by alien crafts. This has been documented in many official reports, photographs and footage obtained by Russian military authorities.

One such photo was taken by officers Ghenadi Korniev and Vassili Zaitsev on January 5, 1992 at the Plasetsk missile center, in which two disc-shaped UFOs were observed hovering over the place.

More evidence can supposedly be found at the base of Kapushtin Yar, located in the region of Zhiktur in Astrakhan, Volgograd, in which there allegedly are several large hangars and an underground facility with several floors, in which Russian scientists would be conducting studies on the technology of captured and crashed alien spacecrafts in the territory of the former Soviet Union and actual Confederacy of Independent States, that were recovered by Russian military forces. Allegedly, this is the main Area 51 type facility in Russia.

Under these lines we are showing a sketch with data on some of the extraterrestrial spacecrafts that the Russian Government keeps at this research center, made by a confidential Russian source, which was delivered to Italian journalist and UFO researcher Constantino Paglialunga in 1997.

It is very possible that the place visited by Fidel Castro, where he saw both the alien spaceship and the alien corpse, was the center in Kapushtin Yar, but this will not be known with certainty until the Cuban leader decides to talk about it.

As former President Fidel Castro opened the door with his recent reflection for the discussion on the topic of extraterrestrial life; would he now reveal, in his own words, the reality of extraterrestrial life visiting us, of which he personally saw evidence during his trip to Russia?

In our view, it would be a great contribution to mankind, as such knowledge would help us to effect a change in our collective consciousness, and perhaps, as a result of that, we would deviate from the path of self destruction in which we currently are.

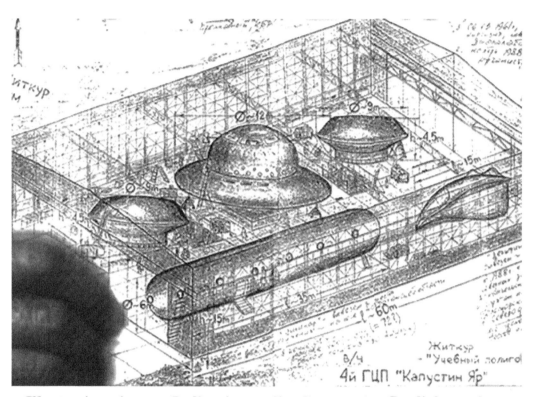

Illustration given to Italian journalist Constantino Paglialunga by a confidential source with the description of some of the alien crafts that were being examined by Russian scientists at the Kapushtin Yar center.

Confronting The Unknown In The Desert Wastes
By Sean Casteel

THE Mojave Desert region of California is a magnet for the strange. In such an inhospitable location, at least for humankind, there nevertheless flourishes a great many UFOs, ghosts and other paranormal manifestations of the unknown that make their presence felt there in no uncertain terms.

Why is there so much interest on the part of otherworldly denizens of the proverbial Twilight Zone? Tim Beckley of Global Communications has recently assembled and released a book called *"Secrets of Death Valley – Mysteries and Haunts of the Mojave Desert"* that tries to answer that question.

Secrets of Death Valley includes dozens of unexplainable mysteries from the heart of the Mojave Desert from the search to find an entrance to the Inner Earth, to reports of albino bigfoot sighted on the perimeter of Edwards Air Force Base, to the incredible tales of other world encounters as told by the late contactee George Van Tassel owner of Giant Rock Airport.

The highly skilled contributors include New Age Channeler Diane Tessman, UFO researcher Regan Lee, fringe topic author Adam Gorightly, as well as Paul Dale Roberts, Joe Parzanese, and a character called Cactus Jim. The lineup is, all in all, an excellent cross-section of experiencers and investigators who work to make the mysteries of the desert a little more accessible.

Regan Lee, for example, writes about the desert as a staging ground for numerous phenomena. "The desert has been the stage," she writes, "for otherworldly encounters with Jinns, Space Visitors, Mary, religious deities and entities." Lee goes on to say that contactee Dana Howard, who met the alien entity Diane there in the Yucca Valley, was no exception to that idea. Diane unequivocally states, "From the desert sands, cauldrons of magic will spring."

It is in that same section of desert that the famous Giant Rock is located, as well as the domed device called the Integratron, a creation of early contactee George Van Tassel. Van Tassel is a major story himself,

134

being one of the first to write about his encounters with alien beings in the early 1950s. Along with the perhaps better known George Adamski, he helped to create much of what we take for granted nowadays about Ufology and other New Age articles of faith.

Beckley has done another of his rescue jobs on the early contactee literature, this time resurrecting a history of Giant Rock written by Van Tassel that has the makings of a great movie. It started with a chance meeting with a traveler named Frank Critzer, who brought his car in for repairs to the auto shop run by Van Tassel's uncle in 1930s Santa Monica, California. Van Tassel and his uncle quickly made friends with Critzer, even allowing him to sleep in their garage and repairing his car for free. When Critzer, an experienced prospector, moved on, he promised to write from wherever he settled down. He left with a $30 gift from Van Tassel and his uncle, a lot of money in those dark days of the Great Depression.

It wasn't until a year later that Critzer was heard from. He sent a map showing how to get to Giant Rock, and the following weekend Van Tassel and his uncle made the trip to see him there. Critzer had made a home for himself by digging out a space under Giant Rock that was surprisingly livable and at least rent free. One needs to realize that Giant Rock covers 5800 square feet and is seven stories high. It is believed to be the largest boulder in the world, and no one can explain how it got to its location so far from any likely point of origin. Critzer's living area was about 400 square feet, a small fraction of the bottom side of Giant Rock.

A former pilot for billionaire Howard Hughes, the late UFO contactee George Van Tassel displays a model of a rejuvenation machine, the plans of which were given to him by the Space Brother. The structure still stands in the town of Landers, Ca.

All was not well for Critzer however. In 1942, when the U.S. was at war with Germany, Critzer was falsely accused of stealing dynamite and failing to register for the draft. He also drew the suspicions of his neighbors, who felt his German name gave away the fact that he was a Nazi spy. Critzer had indeed served in the German Navy many years before, but he had also served in America's Merchant Marines and was a naturalized citizen of the U.S.

Still, deputies from Riverside County came to interrogate him, which is odd, because Giant Rock is actually in San Bernardino County so the Riverside boys had no jurisdiction there, which Critzer pointed out. Critzer agreed to go with them anyway, and said he wanted to get his coat first. He went into his living quarters to retrieve it, but the deputies mistakenly thought he was defying them. They lobbed a tear gas grenade through the north side window, which set off some dynamite that Critzer kept for his prospecting work. Critzer died in the explosion and the deputies were injured.

Van Tassel came to visit Giant Rock in the aftermath of Critzer's death, and he and his family grew to love the place. After the war ended, Van Tassel bought the land from the Bureau of Land Management and built a small airport there. In 1953, Van Tassel began to hold weekly meetings under Giant Rock, which eventually led to his long series of UFO contacts there and to his creation of the Integratron, a device he built on instructions from the aliens that was believed to have regenerative health benefits for humans as well as to make travel in time possible.

Van Tassel's history of Giant Rock is followed by the Global Communications reprint of Van Tassel's contactee classic, *"I Rode A Flying Saucer."* After explaining a little about his own realization that his story was admittedly hard to believe, he next goes on to wax mystical and poetic about the nature of God as creator of the universe, a creator whose work extends far beyond merely earthly mankind.

Helter Skelter

From the sublimely innocent contactees, such as George Van Tassel and Dana Howard, the picture darkens to a shadow of hell with the appearance of Charles Manson and his demonically-inspired madness. Writer Adam Gorightly contributes a chapter that traces the history of Manson's time in the Death Valley region. One of Manson's followers told him about an abandoned mining claim called Myers Ranch, which was one of several desert outposts Manson would lead his followers to in his efforts to conceal himself and his "family" from the imagined horrors of "Helter Skelter," his Beatles-inspired term for the apocalypse.

Manson spent hundreds of dollars on topographic maps of the area to plan an escape route for himself and his cult. The flames of his paranoia were further fanned by his twisted interpretation of the Book of Revelation with the Beatles' White Album thrown into the mix. He believed the Fab Four were in reality angels sent to destroy a third part of mankind and that a total upheaval of the social order was just around the corner.

Manson also believed there was a magic hole located in the desert, spoken of in Hopi legend, which would shelter his group during the apocalypse and permit them to return to the surface once the strife was over. A pit of water called "Devil's Hole," found near the northwest corner of Death Valley, was one possible location of the supernatural escape route. Manson would meditate in front of the hole for days at a time, until it dawned on him that the water in the hole was a door, or a blocking mechanism, that prevented entrance into the underworld. All he needed to do was to somehow suck the water out and the secret passageway would be revealed.

But sorry, Charlie. On the night of October 12, 1969, a contingent of Inyo County sheriff's officers, National Park Rangers and California Highway Patrolmen raided the Manson Family headquarters and took the entire group into custody for the Tate-LaBianca murders.

"Mysteries and Haunts of the Mojave Desert – Secrets of Death Valley" moves on to relate a series of ghost stories and legends that have been handed down through the years, such as the tale of the Serpent-Necked "Canoa," which is Native-American speak for "Canoe." The storyteller, a Santa Rosa Indian, described a boat with a long neck and the head of a beast that turns out to be a Viking ship, with serpent heads at both the bow and the stern, as pictured in the book. The Indian says that seeing the ship was a bad sign, and that to save himself he had needed to leave the area immediately.

Ed Stevens, the writer relaying the Indian's tale, argues for the plausibility of a ship venturing into the area in late spring, when the Colorado River would be flooded and other water-related factors would

THE AUTHENTIC BOOK OF ULTRA-TERRESTRIAL CONTACTS

come into play. But given that the Indian saw a Viking ship, from centuries before, he was most likely experiencing a form of "retro-cognition," which can loosely be defined as crossing over into the past in an almost physical sense, seeing some scene from antiquity, and then returning to the present. The phenomenon has been reported on numerous occasions and is not as rare as some might think.

There are other chapters of a similar nature, with intriguing titles like "Butcher-Knife Ike and the Lost Ship" and "The Lost Spanish Galleon." Beckley also reprints newspaper articles dating back to the 19th century that report on odd occurrences there in the desert, such as one about a group of explorers who discovered yet another ship said to have been lost there many years before.

Giant Skeletons in the Desert

Another chapter, taken from a 1947 article in the San Diego Union, claims that the skeletal remains of several human beings eight to nine feet in height were discovered in the desert near the Arizona-Nevada-California borderline. The giant skeletons were found clothed in garments consisting of a medium-length jacket and trousers that extended to slightly below the knees.

The material was similar to gray dyed sheepskin, but "obviously it was taken from an animal unknown today." The section also includes reporting on the same find from other newspapers at the time, providing a thorough cross section of media coverage of an extremely bizarre and grisly discovery.

Temperatures may well go to over a hundred degrees in death valley, but it doesnt take away from the strange atmosphere noted by those visitors who come in search of the unknown.

Not to be outdone, Tim Beckley himself authors a series of chapters on some high strangeness in the forbidding desert region. For instance, there is his report on a Bigfoot-type creature often sighted near such desert towns as Twenty Nine Palms and Joshua Tree. Even more remarkable is the fact that Bigfoot has been seen frequently in the area around Edwards Air Force Base in the Mojave Desert just north of Lancaster. The presence of Bigfoot became a running joke among the military personnel stationed there, which some at the base connected to the frequent visits made by UFOs to the installation. The Bigfoot/UFO connection has been reported for decades in many other parts of the world as well, and one can only wonder about the relationship the two phenomena apparently have with one another.

Beckley also talks about some ghostly manifestations in a Death Valley hotel and opera house located in a small town called Amargosa, noting that it was not the sort of situation he expected to encounter on his trips to the area. Amargosa was once the location of a borax mine, and was essentially built to be a company town.

"The Amargosa Hotel and Opera House," Beckley explained, "was originally put up for the borax miners and their families, who hadn't much to do in the 1920s. It laid abandoned for years until a woman named Marta Becket arrived from New York and cleaned up the place."

Becket was an accomplished actress, dancer, choreographer and painter. After restoring the Opera House in the 1960s, she began to give one-woman performances there, often without an audience. A lot of paranormal activity has been reported there in the intervening years.

"We drew upon the research," Beckley said, "of Layla Halfhill of the Los Angeles Paranormal Association. Her group scoped out the place really well and noted some abnormalities of a parapsychological nature."

The book contains a haunting photo of an orb taken by the Los Angeles Paranormal Association, who maintain that the Amargosa Hotel and Opera House holds deep mysteries that need further investigation.

Add to that a chapter by Beckley on celebrities who had supernatural encounters in the desert, to include Sammy Davis, Jr., jazz drummer Buddy Rich, and actors William Shatner and Michael Boatman. Beckley also includes a number of other desert anomalies that have become part of the urban legends of the Mojave, such as a twelve-foot-tall levitating clown who is seen to wander down the middle of the road around midnight; a teleporting leprechaun that might direct a worthy party to gold; the repeated apparition of a stagecoach from over a century ago; and a singer who had an "in-your-nose" confrontation with a small orb-like UFO.

In addition, the book is filled with numerous photos, some old and some new, of desert locales and the people whose lives were mysteriously touched there. As mentioned before, there are also numerous newspaper clippings provided that offer further evidence of paranormal events in the area stretching back many years.

Beckley offers a wonderful smorgasbord of several writers making their individual contributions to a book that runs the gamut from the halcyon early days of Giant Rock and the contactee movement to the dark side manifested in the desert rat called Charlie Manson to the many ghostly appearances of the unknown in the barren wastes called Death Valley and the Mojave. By reading "Secrets of Death Valley – Mysteries and Haunts of the Mojave Desert," one can become a kind of tourist of the region without even breaking a sweat and shudder in fear in the privacy of one's own home.

An Interview with Timothy Green Beckley
By Brent Raynes

TIMOTHY Green Beckley, editor, publisher, movie producer, UFO-paranormal-conspiracy researcher, began reading *FATE* magazine back in 1957, at age ten, the same year he sighted two UFOs over his New Jersey home. He hasn't stopped thinking, researching, investigating and writing about the subject of UFOs and things that go "bump in the night" since (he also had some classic paranormal experiences back in his childhood as well) and is today regarded as an internationally acclaimed authority on practically all things strange, unexplained and paranormal.

Read our exclusive interview with Mr. Beckley as he takes us to the beginning of his fascinating and unusual life journey, which has been fifty years since that UFO sighting at age ten, and he brings us up to the present time with his latest efforts and his personal thoughts and reflections on what he has learned over these many years.

* * *

Editor: Your interest in the realms of the supernatural, unexplained phenomena, and UFOs really goes back to your childhood. Living in New Jersey, you grew up in a haunted house with poltergeist phenomena. Could you recount a little about that for us?

Tim Beckley: I guess the paranormal probably came pretty easy for me. My mother had an unusually high level of interest in the subject. I won't say that she was psychic, but she seemed to believe in a lot of this and read a lot of the literature that was available at the time.

Around the age of six, I recall having like poltergeist phenomena occurring spontaneously around the house. Lights would go on and off, doors would open and close. This would not be on a nightly basis. I wouldn't want anybody to think that it was the Amityville Horror. It wasn't by any means, but things did occur from time to time. I remember in particular I was seated at the dinner table and this big dish slid across the table and kind of floated to the floor, and it didn't break. Maybe it didn't break because it was a heavy dish. I don't know. I mean, you could read something into this. Whatever you want. But it occurred.

We also had the peculiar phenomena of a baby crying around the house. I remember one night in the middle of the winter hearing the sound of a baby crying and my mother and I went to the back door, opened it up, and there in the snow, leading down to the few steps to the driveway, was what appeared to be little baby booty prints, and we followed them in the back and they just disappeared in the snow.

My godmother, who was a real staunch Catholic and not prone to believe in any of this stuff at all apparently was there one day and she heard the sound of a baby crying (I guess maybe she had been babysitting me at that point) and opened the door and there was a woman with a baby in her arms, rocking the baby and the baby was crying. My godmother knew that there was no such person in the house (there was only my grandparents) so she got kind of spooked and closed the door, and when she opened it again there was nobody there. Later on we found (I guess my mother and somebody did some research) and we found that there was an incident going back, I don't know what year, but this was during some epidemic, maybe around 1914, 1918. There were thousands of people dying around the world, and apparently a mother and her daughter had died in the house. They had a wake and they put the baby in the same coffin as the mother. So maybe this was the ghost that we were encountering, if it was a ghost indeed. But there were supernatural things happening in the Beckley residence I would certainly say.

The next thing that happened would have been some out-of-body experiences. Maybe at the age of seven or so, where I actually found myself floating in the air (not in my physical body but I guess in my astral form) and I could see that the room was filled with all of these strange colors. I remember seeing vivid colors and hearing celestial music. Don't ask me what it sounded like. I don't remember. But I remember that's what happened at the time, and then a little while later I found myself back in my body, and I actually remember tumbling or being drawn back into it and I awoke in a really, really cold sweat. This happened a few times, and then later on in life I did have some astral projection experiences that were more controlled than this.

Anyway these things were happening, and at the age of ten I had my first of three UFO sightings.

Editor: Right, and I recall from reading a previous interview that even though you were just ten you knew that this was something unusual.

Tim Beckley: Well, with the UFO sighting there was no doubt about it. That's even clearer than any of these other experiences that I just told you about. I've told this story so many times it's almost like repeating a record really, but it was a warm summer evening in 1957. We were all sitting outside because in those days nobody had air conditioning. So we all sat outside until it cooled off. It was just after twilight, as I recall, and somebody had come up the stairs where I was seated with four or five people sitting around chatting, and somebody pointed out these two objects in the sky.

Now I can't tell you that I saw any landing gear. There were no little men and I was not abducted. But there were two bright lights up above the clouds. I would estimate that they were maybe 30-35 feet in diameter, very brightly lit objects, or orbs I guess you'd call them. You can't say objects because I didn't see any metallic hull or anything like that. One of them was across the street over an abandoned factory building and the other one was directly over the house, and they kept rotating in the sky so that the one over the house would go over to where the one over the manufacturing building had been, and that one would move over to the house, and they would kind of like circle overhead. I think this went on for a period of maybe 15 minutes or so, until the one across the street it looked like someone had pulled the light switch because it just disappeared.

The next day there was a little item in the newspaper to the effect that other people had witnessed these lights and the authorities were saying that they were nothing more unusual than weather balloons. Well, even at the rather tend age of ten, it kind of struck me funny because I knew these weren't weather balloons. It wasn't something that was bobbing and weaving in the air current. They were much too large and they did seem to be under intelligent control. So I don't know what they were. I cannot tell you that they were from outer space, but they were up there in the sky. It fascinated me and I remember writing to the newspaper with my concern that the authorities were saying that there was a conventional explanation and I was pretty sure that there wasn't, and that kind of led to my coming out of the closet UFOwise. I started putting out a little newsletter called *The Interplanetary News Service Report* and the first issue I had printed by a fellow by the name of Alan Katz who lived in Middlesex, New Jersey and he had a mimeograph machine and printed like 50 copies of the newsletter, and it was me and a fellow by the name of Edward J. Babcock Jr. who did a book early on called **UFOs Around The World**, and we were the first researchers to actually give credibility to the idea that there were UFO sightings not only in this country but all over the world, and we had contributors from maybe twenty different countries. We printed this book. In those days there were no fast copy places like Kinko, Staples, or any of those other places, so you had to do everything yourself. You either had a ditto machine, which was this terrible liquid like purple. It wasn't even liquid, it was like alkaloid, so that you couldn't print maybe more than 75 copies and then it would evaporate on you, and then the next step up was a mimeograph machine. So I went out and bought a mimeograph machine and Jerry Clark cut my stencils. He was the assistant editor of *The Interplanetary News Service Report*.

Editor: This is the Jerry Clark, known today as Jerome Clark?

Tim Beckley: The Jerry Clark, whether he wants to admit it or not, he cut my stencils, and Lucius Farish was the assistant director of *The Interplanetary News Service Report*, even though Lucius and I have not spoken in years. He did not like the fact that I was associated or friendly with Gray Barker and Jim Moseley. He didn't like Jim Moseley because he had run an expose on George Adamski.

A lot of us active in the field today got started as teenagers. There was a whole confederation of teenaged UFO researchers. Gene Steinberg put out *The UFO Reporter*. I believe that was the name of his publication. He does The Paracast today on the Internet. Allen Greenfield, of course, was a good friend and associate as was Rick Hilberg, or Ricky Hilberg in those days. And so we all kind of got started together.

Editor: Well back in 1967, when I got started I had a little publication called *Sauceritis* which I mimeographed, and I corresponded with Lou

Farish back in those days quite extensively, and Loren Coleman was on my little board of directors. (laughs)

Tim Beckley: Is that right? Huh. Well, we must have been all pretty handsome and pretty young in those days I guess.

Editor: It goes back a ways. Of course, you became active pretty quick. There was Harold Salkin back in the mid-1960s.

Tim Beckley: Harold is one of the unsung heroes in the field. Harold was out of Washington, D.C. He shared the choirs with Clara John who actually ghost wrote Adamski's book *Inside the Spaceships*, and they put out a publication called *The Little Listening Post*, which was a very, very chatty newsletter about maybe six or seven pages. It was kind of like the Paul Harvey of ufology. Everything was broken down real fast, very accurate, and it always seemed that whenever you got *The Little Listening Post* something was going on even if nothing was going on.

Harold, just by synchronicity or coincidence, and of course we know there is no such thing, but anyway his mother lived in the next town over from where I was, in Highland Park, New Jersey, and when he was in town visiting his mother he would call me on the phone and we would chat and we got together, and maybe I was 16 or so at the time. I had this old I guess Remington manual typewriter and we knocked out an article for *Saga* magazine. It was one of the best that I ever wrote which was the astronaut sightings and encounters, long before anybody else was writing about any of this.

Editor: Right. That's been reprinted in your recent book.

Tim Beckley: It's in our book *Strange Saga*. Anyway, Harold and I had gone to the NASA headquarters in Washington, and even though James Oberg has called me a liar on this, we spent three days at NASA headquarters, we went through their files. They were very kind to us. They showed us every single transcript that we wanted to see. We culled out of the printed transcripts, page by page by page, and they also gave us a sheet that stated on top "UFO Photos Taken By The Astronauts." We got prints of all of these things. I wrote an article for *Genesis* magazine, of all places, which is one of the men's magazines. I was a movie review critic for *Hustler* magazine. I don't know if most people realize that. I wrote for a lot of men's magazines in those days, and in *Genesis* I wrote this piece with a lot of photographs that had never been published before that date.

Oberg says that I made it up, but I didn't make this up. I didn't lie. He's just B.S.ing again. He believes what he wants to believe and I know what I know. We didn't make any of that up. All of that testimony of the astronauts and what they saw was right there in the documents.

There were so many UFO groups back in those days. We exchanged publications with 125 different UFO organizations around the world, back when there were actual physical publications.

So anyway, Harold Salkin was not only the co-editor (although they never used their names), he actually helped NICAP get started. He donated I think the first $1000. that NICAP ever saw. He helped Major Keyhoe write that famous *True* article and at the same time he was helping out with the voice of NICAP he was also Adamski's unofficial publicist, Dan Fry, Wayne Aho, and other New Age contactee types. Whenever they came to Washington, Harold would get them on radio and TV. He never got paid doing any of this. Again, there's no money to be made on UFOs per se.

In fact, I remember back during the Vietnam War Era, Harold had booked me in the large YMCA in Washington to give a lecture and I had brought all of my slides down and everything, and it was in the middle of a demonstration and there were five people in the audience. I still went ahead with my lecture. Police had the whole area blocked off and I could see through a big picture window as I was giving the lecture the police were tear-gassing people and people were running in all directions. I said to myself, "Probably some of these people who are running actually came to hear the lecture and were not war protestors." (laughs) I'm sure that out of the 500 or 600 people that were being scurried down the street with the tear gas, I'm sure that there were a couple little old ladies in there who were bent on getting to the Y to hear my talk, but they never made it to the front door. I don't even know how those five people got in, to be honest with you.

Then Harold moved up to New York and we started writing for the tabloids. My publishing company, Global Communications, was a news feature service that supplied articles to magazines and newspapers all over the world. Not just on UFOs but on a lot of different subjects, and the tabloids were our big market. Most of the articles, even though the stories did not contain our name, many of the articles in *The Enquirer*, which were not made up, were written by us. In fact, we had a couple of headline stories in there which we even got pretty large sized bonuses for, back before *The Enquirer* decided that not enough people were interested in UFOs and dropped that from their format to go totally celebrity.

Harold died just recently. He was in the military, you know, during World War II. He was kind of a combat stringer for the Associated Press. That's why when he got out of the military he knew all of these guys who worked for Voice of America. I actually was on a show that had the potential audience of a 130 million listeners on the Voice of America, and they actually had programs on UFOs. Many were censoring it in this country but we got to talk all about this stuff and it went out all over the world.

Editor: Did you ever meet Bob Pratt?

Tim Beckley: You know, I don't know if I did or not. We were stringers, free-lancers. We did have a pretty close relationship with the Enquirer people down in Florida and went by there a couple of times. My main contact was a fellow by the name of Cliff Linedecker, who actually wrote a couple of books on psychic phenomena, including I believe a book on country western singers who had metaphysical experiences, ghost encounters, and so forth.

I met a number of the people there, but I don't know if I ever met Bob Pratt. I did correspond with him and, of course, I sold his book. His book **UFO Danger Zone** was certainly a very well researched volume. One of the best, I would say, in the field, although I don't necessarily agree with his conclusions that UFOs are menacing or hostile. It seems like a handful of sightings out of tens or thousands of reports don't necessarily make an accurate conclusion.

I will say one thing. People think that *The Enquirer* was yellow journalism and that they made up stories. They never made up anything that I am certainly aware of.

I remember being at a MUFON Conference, one of the few that I've ever gone to, and Tracy Torme was there, and of course Tracy did *Fire In*

The Sky and his father was Mel Torme, the famous singer. I had written an article about Torme's UFO sighting, which was not particularly spectacular. He was out walking his dog near Central Park one day and there was an object in the sky, and I mentioned that to Tracy as a way of introducing myself and he said, "My dad said that was the most accurate article ever written about him." All *The Enquirer* ever did was use exact quotes. We would provide them with the tapes of the interviews, with the witnesses, and pretty much all that they would do was take the quoted material. There was very little introduction, very little between any paragraphs. It was just stated word for word, none of it was made up, despite what other UFO researchers, who are not in the know about most things, would have you believe.

People ask me, "What do you think UFOs are?" I say, "Well UFOs are unidentified. It doesn't necessarily even have to be flying, and there's probably more than one phenomenon." It's obvious that we're not talking about one thing here. Brad Steiger has his list of 17 different UFO origins and theories, so I'm sure that some are spiritual phenomena, some physical craft from other planets (although I don't think there are many of those here, but maybe every once and awhile). Then others of them are intelligently controlled earth lights. I have written about this, and you've written about this as well, and I wrote about this subject extensively in my book *Our Alien Planet: This Eerie Earth*.

Editor: Right, it could be earth energies or Keel's old ultraterrestrials.

Tim Beckley: That seems to be a popular explanation or theory these days and a lot of people are taking credit for it, not realizing other people who came before them. Allen Greenfield should actually get quite a bit of credit. I remember doing an interview with him for Ray Palmer's magazine. He was one of the first to talk about alternate realities or other dimensions.

Editor: It's amazing how many of the current crop of ufologists don't even know when you mention John Keel or Jacques Vallee or Allen Greenfield who you're talking about.

Tim Beckley: Well, I would hope that they would know who John Keel is.

Editor: Well, of course, after the movie came out you do have more people, and he also went on Art Bell, but before that a lot of people really didn't know.

Tim Beckley: I think I'm one of the few people who talks to John every other week or so, but we don't talk that much about UFOs. We've been kind of personal friends over the years.

Editor: He's certainly presented a lot of very interesting data and I've talked to him on the phone a few times too.

Tim Beckley: He doesn't like to give interviews.

Editor: No, he doesn't. You have to settle for a little comment here and there that he might let you share but not an interview.

Tim Beckley: I guess he figures he's interviewed out. Whatever he's said he's said many times.

Editor: Yeah, he's told me to go get one that has already been published and re-use that.

Tim Beckley: I guess another great influence in my career as a writer and publisher was Gray Barker. Gray published Saucerian Publications out of Clarksburg, West Virginia, and of course Gray was best known for his book, *They Knew Too Much About Flying Saucers*. Now I believe that it was in the 5th or 6th grade that I had to do a book review, and what book did I pick. It was, They Knew Too Much About Flying Saucers, of course not knowing at that point that Gray would be the publisher of my first book and that after he passed away I would buy from his estate the remainder of the copies of that particular title. It impressed me not only because of its contents but also because of his writing style, and I always wanted to write like Gray Barker (laughs) and I guess that some would say that I accomplished that, for better or for worse, or whatever.

And for some reason, which I can't remember off hand, at one point he wasn't doing a column anymore. I wrote to Ray Palmer and said I'd like to do my own column, and so in the late 1960s I started doing a regular column for *Flying Saucers* magazine called *On The Trail Of The Flying Saucers*, which ran for maybe five or six years. Then I did a couple of columns for *Search* magazine, which was one of Palmer's other publications. Of course, Ray was the man who kind of started UFOs and was responsible for the Shaver mystery. I became fairly friendly at least in correspondence with Richard Shaver. He was a character, as everybody knows, and people ask me, "Well, what is the truth about Richard Shaver's claims," and I just look at them and say, "I don't know." Obviously, the inner earth and the whole idea of a subterranean world holds a great fascination with people.

In fact, people don't realize this but being in the UFO publishing business like I am there are more books sold that deal with UFOs being of Nazi origin and originating from the inner earth. People are not interested in UFOs from outer space.

Editor: Oh really?

Tim Beckley: That is the least popular theory. In fact, any time that I have tried to publish anything serious, and any time I have gotten a good review in The MUFON Journal I know that is the kiss of death as far as book sales go. Of course, there have obviously been some exceptions, like the Betty and Barney Hill book, The Interrupted Journey and some of Frank Edwards's early books, but those are few and far between.

Editor: That's just the opposite of what I would have thought.

Tim Beckley: Well there you go. I've certainly published my share of what I would consider serious UFO books. One of my favorites was by Jenny Randles, *From Out Of The Blue*, about Bentwaters, the UFO landing at the NATO base there and the contact and so forth with the US military, and we sold the paperback rights and the book just barely paid off in very small advances and sold less than 15,000 copies in paperback, which is why publishers do not publish UFO books because they just don't sell in big numbers.

With a few exceptions over the years, UFO books don't sell in big numbers. So they don't publish them. It's not a censorship thing. It's a bottom line.

Editor: And it's been that way for a long time.

Tim Beckley: Yeah, a long time. The coming of Barnes and Noble and Amazon destroyed the middle level publisher. Guys like me, who would have a new title and would print two or three thousand copies, a very small run, but we had wholesalers who would distribute them and we had over 3000 mom and pop metaphysical/New Age/alternative stores around the country who would scoop these things up. They would never sell more than a couple of copies of each title, but there were a lot of them, but little by little they went out of business, and today there are very few left. Very few wholesalers and distributors who specialize in this type of thing and not very many stores anymore, and the stores that are still around their income is mainly derived from selling crystals and incense and such.

Editor: Yeah, I saw a real nice crystal in one of those stores recently for about $2000.

Tim Beckley: Oh yeah, some of them are really high priced, but some of them are museum quality pieces. They're really nice. Even in the mail order business, that's what people seem to want. That's what they're looking to buy. They don't want a serious book on UFOs.

Editor: Now you were involved with many people who were involved in the forming of the Congress of Scientific Ufologists, and of course one of the biggest ones was in New York City back in 1967.

Tim Beckley: I was indeed Jim Moseley's assistant with that, and I actually introduced Roy Thinnes to the audience. He was of course the star of the TV show The Invaders about aliens invading the earth.

Editor: I remember that show well. I used to watch it every night it was on.

Tim Beckley: Yeah, it was pretty good program, and Roy came down, Jim paid his expenses. Most people don't realize this. They think Jim made a lot of money on that, but he broke even, because a lot of people ended up getting in for free. Things got screwed up and the elevator was opening up on the wrong floor and people were coming in by the droves and not paying the big admission of two dollars.

There were quite a variety of speakers like Venus from the planet Venus, Dr. Frank Stranges, Howard Menger, and in fact Dr. Condon of the infamous Condon Report was there. He was in the audience taking notes.

Editor: And of course John Keel was there.

Tim Beckley: Now that's pretty funny. John Keel was to give a talk at a closed session to Jim's group, the Inner Circle, and people think that there is a kind of bootleg tape that people have passed around of John's lecture at that conference, but what most people don't realize is that it was broadcast on the radio, on WBAI, so it really wasn't a secret lecture because probably thousands of people heard it on the radio.

Editor: Oh, so this tape I've got over here on the shelf wasn't an exclusive after all. I have a tape I think Al Greenfield supplied me with years ago of a talk that Keel gave at that conference.

Tim Beckley: There were about 12,000 people who attended that conference. The hotel held about maybe 2,200 people. Long John Nebel, the original all night talk show host, had a UFO speaker on every night for a week before the show. He really packed 'em in and drew in the people in those days. If you were a speaker on the Long John Show you could pretty much be assured of a pretty good turnout the next day, or whenever the lecture was going to be. In those days it was a pretty spectacular show, a lobby full of vendors, book sellers, and artifacts of one type or another.

Editor: You were a regular there for quite awhile on the Long John Nebel Show.

Tim Beckley: Somebody just sent me a listing for the *New York Times* of 1965 of an appearance that I made on The Amazing Randi's program. Now most people don't realize, or care to realize, that with Long John's switch from WOR to, I believe it was WNBC they needed somebody to take Long John's place, and so for about two years The Amazing Randi was host of an all night talk show there. His program was not devoted to the paranormal and UFOs, though he did do some programs on the subject. The only thing was that if you went on Randi's program Long John would not let you on his show, so for quite a few years some of us were kind of blacklisted. We couldn't do Long John. But then after awhile, when Randi went off the air, it didn't matter too much.

Editor: Then, of course, there were the celebrities.

Tim Beckley: There were two reasons that I got around to doing the celebrity interviews. As I said I was a stringer for *The Enquirer*, so I met all of these celebrities and in those days they were not just interested in

Courtney Love and Britney Spears and Brad Pitt. They covered many celebrities, including those who were relatively obscure and hadn't done anything in awhile. We did people lots and lots of people, and of course one of the questions I always asked a lot of the celebrities was, "Have you ever had a UFO sighting?" "Have you ever lived in a haunted house or experienced anything supernatural?" And a lot of them did.

Bill Shatner told me a story about having a UFO encounter in the Mojave Desert where a UFO appeared overhead. I guess that he got separated from a motor cycle group that he was with. He was all dressed in leather and had a helmet on and it was like in the middle of the afternoon, 102 degrees, and the motorcycle conked out, and the UFO appeared overhead and led him out of the desert. Kind of like a Moses trip or something. (laughs)

Editor: I always wondered if that was a true story there.

Tim Beckley: Well, that's the story he told me. He told it to me backstage at the Ten Thousand Dollar Pyramid, which is where I did the interview with him, and somewhere here on an audio tape I still have it. Some people have heard it, and other people have lifted the story, and all of these stories have made the rounds.

Editor: Also David Bowie?

Tim Beckley: You see, I promoted quite a few rock and roll shows and met quite a few of those stars back in those days. My friend Walli Elmlark was the White Witch of New York, and she also wrote a column for Circus magazine which is kind of a hard rock version of Rolling Stones. She met all of these different rock stars and I would hang out at her apartment and since I was writing for some of the magazines too I met them at press conferences and socialized with them. Of course, this is when they were on their way up the ladder to success although they were more anxious to meet with the press and tell their stories and all. And when I did meet with David he was signed to RCA Records and he was doing the Ziggy Stardust tour. I met him and he was dressed up as Ziggy Stardust. We never did talk a great deal about UFOs. He did tell me that he believed in UFOs and was interested in the aliens and stuff like that, but he was good friends with Walli and in one of the books written about David Bowie's career there is three pages about Walli's dealings with him because for awhile he was heavily into the Wicca. Then he got into Buddhism, and I don't know what he's into now. But rumor has it that he had UFO sightings in England while growing up and then was actually an editor of a UFO newsletter when he was a teenager, but I don't know what that newsletter was.

Editor: And then May Pang, who was John Lennon's former girlfriend.

Tim Beckley: At one point with May Pang, we did a couple of radio shows discussing John Lennon's UFO sighting up on The Dakota, because she was living with him at the time and they were both naked on the balcony overlooking Manhattan. He called her out to the balcony and they watched these strange lights in the sky. It was a UFO over Manhattan.

I talked to John Lennon a couple of times on the phone. There was a band that was his back up band that was called Elephant's Memory and we had a Halloween Concert and an occult program at the Hotel Diplomat, which is where Kiss did their first show, and John Lennon showed up, and Andy Warhol. It was a pretty good party, and I guess he came because Elephant's Memory were our headliners. I didn't get to talk with him, but I did see him there. But when I did get to talk with him on the phone he was very much into this fellow by the name of Dean Kraft who had some psychokinetic ability similar to Uri Geller. He could move objects across the room, and Yoko Ono and John told me about how he had apparently passed his hand over this candy dish that was on their coffee table and a couple of pieces of candy came over the top of the candy dish and kind of squiggled out until they fell onto the floor.

There was a big article written about Kraft in, of all places, I think it was *Cosmopolitan* magazine. He was very well known at that time, and he was written up in *The Enquirer* and he had quite a notoriety for doing psychic healing. He was very well known for that. He moved down to Florida. I went to his wedding. I haven't been in touch with him for years, but I believe he's still in Florida and still doing healing work. He also wrote a book.

Editor: I know that John Lennon had also met with Uri Geller in New York.

Tim Beckley: Well you know Uri and I were fairly good friends. I had an office just off of Central Park and Uri around the corner a couple of blocks away and he had just landed here in the United States and was looking for publicity, and so we did a couple of articles for *Saga* magazine and a couple of the papers and weeklies in Manhattan.

I saw him do a couple of things that I thought was fairly incredible. I was in his apartment one time with the science editor of *Argosy* magazine. Now *Argosy* magazine was one of these men's adventure publications. Real little cheesecake, but basically articles about people's wartime experiences, or kind of He man stuff I guess you'd call it.

The science editor of *Argosy* was a fellow by the name of Herbert Bailey, who was a pretty good friend of mine. But anyway I had introduced Herb to Uri (we were in either Herb's apartment or Uri's, I forget for certain) but he told Herb to hold his key in his hand and told me to take my key and put it on the desk across the room, and he said, "Let's see what happens." So he started stroking the key that Herb had in his hand. It was no slight of hand trick. He didn't change the key out. It was Herb's key to his front door. In fact, I remember later on he was kind of upset because he couldn't use it in the door anymore. The thing bent about I would say about a little bit more than a third of the way. After they were finished doing this, Uri said, "Take a look at your key across the room." I picked it up from the desk and it was bent a little bit. Not as much as Herb's was, but it definitely had a little bit of curl to that tip.

Mohammed Ali was a big UFO buff actually. We went down to his home at Cherry Hill and he wanted us to bring slides and movies, because he wanted to see if it was like anything he had seen in the sky.

He claimed over twenty-one sightings and he tied it in with his religious beliefs. I first met him after the Daily News ran a report about Mohammed Ali sighting two bright lights over Central Park while he was out jogging one morning. Harold was a big promoter and he'd get on the phone and call anybody and Harold got Angelo Dundee on the phone and said, "We'd like to come around and talk to the Champ about his UFO sightings." So Dundee said, "Well he's out there jogging through the park around 6 a.m. Come and join him." So we got out there at 6 a.m. and I was in a little better shape in those days and jogged maybe a quarter of a mile with the Champ and he told me about his UFO sightings and so forth, and invited us down to his home in Cherry Hill. We went there a couple of times to show him the UFO movies and pictures, whatever he wanted, and he even did a drawing for us, which I've used in my book, *UFOs Among The Stars*, of one of the UFOs that he had seen which looks exactly like an Adamski craft. I think he was into the Adamski ships in those days. He must have seen an Adamski photo or two or read an Adamski book and that was his cup of tea. He had also seen this huge mother ship parked up above his training camp in Deer Park, Pennsylvania. He invited us up to see if we could see it as well, which we never did, but also took Uri Geller with us. Ali was at first interested in meeting Geller, but Ali is the type of person who is not going to share the spotlight with anyone, even if there's only three people around he's the one who wants the attention, and I can't say that Uri is too much different than that either. He likes a little bit of attention as well as all of us do, you know.

Anyway we took Uri up there and Ali knew who he was. I guess he had seen him on the Johnny Carson Show. It turned out that Ali is an amateur magician so he got his tricks out, like the one where you cut the rope in half and you magically put it back together, and a couple of other tricks with a ring and such that I don't remember exactly, but Uri got a little bit peeved at that because he thought that maybe Ali was trying to put him down. So we kind of slipped away from the main group and went over to this big rock where he (Ali) would stand up on the rock or next to the rock and ring a bell that was on the rock when he wanted people to gather around. Anyway, there was a guy there who was Ali's sparing partner, and I wrote this up in *UFOs Among The Stars* and in *The Enquirer*, and I had a photo of the guy, but anyway this sparing partner of Ali's had this medallion around his neck like a St. Jude or St. Christopher's medal. It was pretty heavy. It wasn't a cheap medal. It was a piece of silver. So Uri takes his thumb and he pushes his thumb into the medal and takes it away maybe two or three seconds later and there's an impression in the guy's medal, like he had indented it with his thumb.

That seemed to be a little bit beyond a little magic trick. He didn't take the medal off of the guy's neck or anything like. He just pressed it and there's an indention in the medal obvious for all to see.

Then Melinda Ali, who I believe was Ali's second wife, was curious about this more so than Ali seemed to be that day and Uri did an experiment with her where he took his hand and put it over a ring that she was wearing, and I couldn't tell you exactly what kind of a ring it was. I don't think it was an expensive diamond or anything like that. He put his hand over it and started kind of touching on her hand, but nothing too overt. He wasn't touching the stone. He didn't have any utensils in his hand or anything like that, and then after a few seconds he said "Let me know if you feel anything strange or anything different," and then after a few seconds into it she said, "Ouch, my hand is getting warm," and then a few more seconds after that he took his hand away, the ring itself was still there but the stone inside the setting was gone. So how he accomplished that I don't know, and as far as I know she never got the stone back. She seemed pretty awed by that.

So is he an entertainer? Yes, in his own way. Is he a magician? No, I think whatever he's doing he's pretty legitimate about it. Maybe not a hundred percent of the time, but whenever I saw him I don't think that there was any overt attempt to create a fraud there.

Editor: Now back in your travels, back in the 1960s, you went to one of the better known windows, or UFO sighting locations, over in Warminster, England, where you met Arthur Shuttlewood, and that was when you saw one of your other UFOs.

Tim Beckley: That would have been my second of three UFO sightings. I was invited by my friend Brinsley La Poer Trench who wrote the book *The Sky People*, and a book on the inner earth, which we have in print now. He was an interesting character, and in fact he was a member of the House of Lords and he was responsible for trying to get a little bit of interest going with the members of the British Parliament to get them to release whatever information that might be available on UFOs. This was long before Nick Pope.

Anyway, they organized a UFO study group made up of members of Parliament and the House of Lords, people like Lord Hill Norton who was the former head of the British Fleet, a former Admiral. I was invited over to deliver a talk to the group, and then afterwards, after giving this little address I got to meet everybody and shake hands, I took a little side trip out into the country and went to Stonehenge, and not far from there is the town of Warminster where Arthur Shuttlewood was the editor of the daily newspaper there, *The Warminster Journal*. This was, of course, the seat of all UFO activity in England at that time. Hundreds of sightings, including I think Mick Jagger was one of those who had observed something in the sky hovering over Cradle Hill, and Starr Hill was another area that people would gather to witness these sights. It was quite a remarkable phenomenon that was happening there.

I met with Shuttlewood and we went out to the field at Starr Hill where a lot of these sightings were taking place. It must have been about 11 o'clock in the evening and almost directly overhead. He says, "Here's one of them now." What could I tell you. It looked pretty much like a street lamp in the sky. We were five or six miles out of town and nothing around there. It didn't appear to be moving around or doing anything peculiar, and that's probably why it didn't really catch my attention, but Arthur having witnessed probably dozens if not hundreds of sightings said that this was one of these objects. So he said, "Let's see what will happen." He goes to the trunk of his car and picks up a big torchlight. Not a little flashlight but a big torchlight and starts blinking at the object. Now it wasn't in Morse Code or anything like that. I don't even think he knew Morse Code. But every time that we would blink at this object in the sky it would seem to do a little bit of a somersault or tumble around, as if it were acknowledging our presence in our trying to signal to it with this light. This went on ten minutes or so, if I remember correctly, and then clouds came over and we didn't see the object, and then we eventually left. It was a pretty cloudy night.

In the history of UFOs, many of these intelligent lights whether ghost lights or whatever, they do seem to be responsive to humans who attempt to communicate or signal to them. This is something again I cannot tell you that it was a ship from outer space, but it was something that seemed to acknowledge our presence and our effort to try and signal to it. There was another fellow there who was a retired World War II Air Force pilot by the name of Bob Strong. Now Bob set his camera equipment up there at Starr Hill and Cradle Hill, on a tripod, and this guy had a huge photo album of all kinds of UFOs. I mean, bat shaped things, a whole string of objects going across the sky, cigar shaped craft, and he had photographs of these things, and you know what the darned thing was half of the photo album was missing because someone would say, "Let me borrow that photo. I want to make a copy of it. I'll give it back to you," and so it just depleted his collection in no time. But an amazing collection of photographs, some of which were published in Shuttlewood's various books.

Editor: Wow, what a story. Lots of stories!

Tim Beckley: Yeah, lots of stories.

Editor: So your ultimate conclusion of it all is that there is no one single theory.

Tim Beckley: Yes, that is what I'd have to say. My conclusion is that there is no one conclusion, and there probably never will be a conclusion. I've been doing this, gosh, I wrote my first *FATE* magazine article I think in 1962. I bought my first issue of *FATE* in 1957. I would have been ten years old. I read all of the books by Keyhoe, and I guess that I was impressed enough to start a career, you know? It's been a career that's had it's ups and downs.

And people have to realize, and I don't think that a lot of people do, that I have my own personal opinion on all of these things which means that it happens to coincide with the books and ideas that I publish, because basically I'm a publisher, a successful publisher, and that's what publishers do, even if they don't happen to agree with the content of all of their titles. This is something that most people can't seem to get through their head, that just because I publish a book by somebody who says he was visited by beings from Alpha Centauri or something, it doesn't necessarily mean that I think they were from Alpha Centauri, but I think that there is a need for publishing a book that other people have written about these experiences and let the readers sort it out for themselves. So my conclusion is that there is no conclusion.

Also we hear about Disclosure. There is no disclosure and there will not be a disclosure. The only way that there will be a disclosure is if these objects land and make themselves known. There is not going to be any release of any information from the White House or the Air Force or any other military or governmental group because I don't think that they've really reached any conclusion on this. If you go back and read a lot of the famous things that happened the military is made up by a lot of people who believe and who disbelieve just like there is in civilian life.

Editor: Right. I remember John Keel some thirty years or so ago writing that he felt that the military was just as perplexed by the phenomenon as we were.

Tim Beckley: Is there anything to MJ-12? There might have been some people in the early days of the subject who thought that they had to adopt such tactics, but I doubt if anyone is around today who is aware of any of this information. Maybe higher up in the CIA they had access to certain data and certain reports that haven't been released yet, but what kind of reports would it be. We know that these things have hovered over missile silos, they've interrupted computers, electrical devices, and so everything you see in Close Encounters and science fiction genre has happened in real life. So we know that this stuff goes on, so what's the difference if we have another half dozen sightings over military bases where these things have screwed up our radar or something like that.

There's more evidence to indicate what they are than where they originate from. They could originate from anywhere. A lot of them could be just environmental phenomena.

I have always been attracted to the Native American cultures. Over the years a high percentage of my lady friends have been Native Americans and of course there have been many UFO encounters on various reservations both in U.S. and Canada. (Photo by Charla)

Jimi Hendrix: Starchild

"**I** can't say in all honesty that I really knew Jimi Hendrix, but I did see him give a number of really good performances. It was at one of those post- Woodstock concerts where I managed to wind my way backstage. Jimi Hendrix was leaning up against a wall of amps and speakers. As I walked past him, we both just kind of nodded as if we recognized each other, and to this day I can swear I heard him ask me, 'and what planet are you from pal?'"

Jimi Hendrix fits perfectly some of the characteristics often representative of 'Walk-Ins'.

World traveler Bill Cox has investigated any number of cases involving beings who have come here from other worlds and with the permission of a human, transplanted their spirits inside one of us (usually at the moment of death, just after an accident).

There are emissaries among us who know who they are. They know they are quite different from average men. They may even be misfits in the physical world...I find that among this group, some become excessively involved with alcohol, drugs and sex; anything to try and escape from this, our world. Jimi Hendrix could easily be placed into this category; nobody would deny that.

Jimi expressed a great interest in matters of an extraterrestrial nature, had admitted seeing UFOs, and once told a reporter from The New York Times that he was really from Mars. And he wasn't kidding either. David Henderson, in his book The Life of Jimi Hendrix (Bantam), quotes Jimi's feelings about life on other planets: "There are other people in the solar system, you know, and they have the same feelings too, not necessarily bad feelings, but see, it upsets their way of living for instance - and they are a whole lot heavier than we are."

"And it's no war games, because they all keep the same place. But like the solar system is going through a change soon and it's going to affect the Earth in about 30 years."

On several occasions during his career, UFOs just happened to show up while Jimi was giving a concert. During the last days of his life, he performed on the rim of an extinct volcano in Maui.

Jimi played three 45-minute sets, says Henderson in his best-seller. After each set, he retired to a special sacred Hopi Indian tent. Later, witnesses in Maui testified that they heard musical tones emanating from rocks and stones. UFOs were also sighted over the volcano by people who called in to a local radio show. A cameraman on the set said that he fell from his perch after seeing a UFO through his lens.

In the film Rainbow Bridge, Hendrix rattles on for several minutes about astral projection and the philosophy of the Space Brothers. He also tried to master the art of psychic healing, through color and sound.

Fellow musician and songwriter, Curtis Knight, knew all about the episode involving the UFO in Maui. It was an odd-looking craft that glittered in the bright sunlight. Jimi felt certain the UFO had come down to put its spiritual stamp of approval on the show. He told me that he had been emotionally and physically recharged by the experience.

During the course of our conversation, Curtis also revealed the fascinating details of the time a UFO landed in front of them and actually saved their lives.

The event took place on a cold winter's night near Woodstock, NY in 1965. According to Curtis, if it hadn't been for the occupants of this metallic stranger, Jimi and his fellow musicians might have frozen to death.

It was four o'clock in the morning, and we were trying to make it back to Manhattan - a drive of more than 100 miles - through the worst blizzard I can recall. The wind was whipping the snow around our van so fiercely that we missed the turn-off leading to the state highway that would put us in the direction of home. The next thing I remember is getting stuck in a drift that reached the hood of our vehicle. Soon it got so cold. The windows were rolled up tight, and we had the heater on full blast to protect us from the rawness of the elements. I had my doubts about seeing the light of day. We could have turned to human icicles very easily. That's how bitter it was!

Curtis says the road in front of them suddenly lit up, as a bright phosphorescent object cone-shaped, like a space capsule landed in the snow about 100 feet up ahead. It stood on tripod landing gear, and for all purposes gave the appearance of being something right out of science fiction. At first, we thought it was an apparition caused by the cold and our confused state of mind. I mean, we just couldn't believe our eyes.

Prodding Jimi with his elbow, Curtis asked if his imagination was playing tricks on him or whether the rock star saw it too. Jimi didn't answer, but sort of smiled. He seemed to be staring out into the night, his eyes riveted on this thing resting within a stone's throw.

Curtis was overcome with fright. Before he could make a move of any kind, a door opened on the side of the craft and an entity came forth. He stood eight foot tall, his skin was yellowish, and instead of eyes, the creature had slits. His forehead came to a point, and his head ran straight into his chest, leaving the impression that he had no neck.

The being proceeded to float to the ground and glided toward the trapped occupants of the van. It was then that Curtis noticed the snow was melting in the wake of the creature. His body generated tremendous heat, so much so that as it came across a small rise, the snow disappeared around in all directions. In a matter of what seemed like seconds, the being came over to the right- hand side of the van where Jimi was seated and looked right through the window. Jimi seemed to be communicating telepathically with it.

Curtis relates that immediately the interior of their vehicle began to heat up. "Suddenly, I was roasting! One moment it had been bitter cold, and the next moment we might as well have been in Haiti." The heat coming from the being evaporated the snow enough to free their imprisoned van.

As it glided behind our van, I saw the drift had completely vanished. Turning on the ignition key, I gunned the motor and got out of there. As I looked back through the rear view window, I could see the road filling in with snow again. The object - the strange craft - was at the same instant lifting off like a rocket from a launching pad.

Jimi never did talk much about what happened. He sort of let me know that the cool thing to do was not to bring up the subject. It was to be our little secret. However, from what he did say, I sort of suspect that the object arrived to save our necks chiefly because Jimi had been practicing trying to communicate by ESP with the beings on board. I know this may be hard to believe, but I'm putting it straight, just like it happened, you hear!

The boys from the group who were with us remember nothing. They were out cold in the back. As we got into the main road, they revived. It is as if they had been placed under a spell - you know - hypnotized.

A capsule review of Jimi's songs shows that he incorporated some of his interplanetary ties in with his music. The lyrics of many of his songs contain veiled references to UFOs. His album, Axis-Bold as Love, opens with an announcer talking about flying saucers, with a cut following being a catchy tune called, 'Up From the Stars'.

Though he has passed from this plane, it wouldn't be hard to imagine that somewhere "out there," Jimi isn't watching over earth and smiling and we certainly do miss this vibrant star child who was once in our midst.

David Bowie, UFOs, Witchcraft, Cocaine and Paranoia

BORN David Robert Jones, I first met David Bowie during his original tour of the United States having adapted the stage persona of Ziggy Stardust, a sort of lost in space androgynous alien, complete with cosmic makeup and a painted lightning bolt zig-zaging across his face down to his naked chest.

Before venturing across the pond, Bowie had caused quite a sensation in the British press not only because of his outlandish - to some - image of a rock and roller from Mars, but because of his independent and very liberal sexual lifestyle.

Bowie was introduced to me at the RCA studios in Manhattan by Walli Elmlark a bedazzling young lady who wrote a regular column for Circus magazine, a sort of heavy metal version of Rolling Stone that was printed on glossy paper with color photos of pop star favorites, emerging on the then burgeoning glam and glitter rock scenes.

As usual, at the time I was wearing several hats. I was promoting a number of local rock bands who never quite "made it," editing the widely distributed UFO Review (the world's only official flying saucer newspaper), and running the New York School Of Occult Arts and Science, among the first metaphysical centers in the country where you could take classes in anything from astral projection to hypnosis, to witchcraft...which is how I came to be acquainted with Walli Elmlark.

As I originally wrote in *UFOs Among The Stars - Close Encounters of The Famous* (Global Communications), Wallie was known widely as the White Witch Of New York. Because of her contacts in the music industry, she had established quite an eclectic clientele for whom she would offer spiritual guidance, and occasional good luck or love spells, but always of a positive nature. She didn't dabble in black magick or even gris gris (a New Orleans form of "gray magick" that incorporates poppets and the use of talismans kept in a personal mojo bag). Walli was lively, imaginative, energetic, well spoken, and quite attractive in her flowing white garments complete with fashionable silver moon adornments. Oh did I forget to mention long black hair, complete with dyed green streak highlights?

Indeed, Walli made a very bold fashion and occult statement wherever she went.

Bowie – The Man Who Fell to Earth

Early in life, Bowie had established his interest in all matters extraterrestrial. As a Brit teenager, David had helped edit a flying saucer newsletter. He admitted to me that he loved science fiction and was fascinated with life in space and the possibility that quite a few cosmic visitors had ended up on our earthly shores.

During a conversation, Bowie had gone out on a limb revealing that he had once had a close encounter. In the book *Laugh Gnostic*, author Peter Koening paraphrases what Bowie said: "A friend and I were traveling in the English countryside when we both noticed a strange object hovering above a field. From then on I have come to take this phenomena seriously. I believe that what I saw was not the actual object, but a projection of my own mind trying to make sense of this quantum topological doorway into dimensions beyond our own. It's as if our dimension is but one among an infinite number of others."

In the February 1975 issue of the long defunct *Cream* magazine, Bowie seems to admit to a reporter that he might have an implant or metal inside his body. It's hard to define his exact feeling on this, but this is the quote attributed to him by Bruno Stein the writer who conducted the interview:

"Well, it turned out David was in luck. If he went to a little town in Missouri at a certain time, he would be able to see in a seemingly empty field a fully equipped flying saucer repair shop at work.

"It was one of those fascinating things you learn at a Bowie soiree. This evening the gathering was rather intimate. There was Corinne, David's charming personal secretary, who ducked out early due to exhaustion (although another participant gossiped that she had someone interesting waiting for her in her hotel room)..."I used to work for two guys who put out a UFO magazine in England," he told the flying saucer man. "About six years ago. And I made sightings six, seven times a night for about a year when I was in the observatory. We had regular cruises that came over. We knew the 6.15 was coming in and would meet up with another one. And they would be stationary for about half an hour, and then after verifying what they'd been doing that day, they'd shoot off.

"But I mean, it's what you do with the information. We never used to tell anybody. It was beautifully dissipated when it got to the media. Media control is still based in the main on cultural manipulation. It's just so easy to do. When you set up one set of objectives toward the public and you've given them a certain definition for each code word, you hit them with the various code words and they're not going to believe anything if you don't want them to..."

From his performances, you could tell that nothing was too "non establishment" for David. He incorporated time machines and space capsules into his act and wrote a Space Oddity and talked about how a Starman would like to come and visit us, "but he knows he'd blow our minds." His appearance in the motion picture *The Man Who Fell To Earth* has become a classic. In concert, Bowie was radiant and his fans were floating on a cloud, but behind the scenes an ominous specter was forming from which the master of time and space would quickly need some rightist assistance in order to escape a wall of paranoia that was building around him.

And Along Comes Mr. Scratch

Like many rockers before and after, David had taken a liking to the good life. You know the old adage sex, drugs and rock and roll, well on top of this add a heap of consciousness expansion, an interest in the occult, and you will have the prevalent influences on what might have seemed like Bowie's immortal being. But paranoia soon struck in the form of the ole nemesis "nose candy" commonly known as cocaine.

With the help of Bowie himself and some close associates at the time, Marc Spitz details in the just published Bowie biography (Crown) how David was living in LA just a few houses away from the LaBianca estate where Charlie Manson's gang had terribly mutilated Sharon Tate and her friends in a ritualistic murder. Bowie had taken to doing blow regularly and was getting more and more desperate and paranoid with each passing day.

In a number of shocking revelations, Marc Spitz in the Bowie biography explains precisely what was transpiring in the pop singer's troubled life. "While planning the follow-up to Young Americans (album), Bowie would sit in the house with a pile of high-quality cocaine atop the glass coffee table, a sketch pad and a stack of books. *Psychic Self Defense* (Dion Fortune) was his favorite. Its author describes the book as a 'safeguard for protecting yourself against paranormal malevolence.'

"Using this and more arcane books on witchcraft, white magic and its malevolent counterpart, black magic, as rough guides to his own rapidly fragmenting psyche, Bowie began drawing protective pentagrams on every surface."

Bowie told the author, "I'd stay up for weeks. Even people like Keith Richards were floored by it. And there were pieces of me all over the floor. I paid with the worst manic depression of my life. My psyche went through the roof, it just fractured into pieces. I was hallucinating 24 hours a day."

Spitz adds, "Increasingly Bowie was convinced there were witches after his semen. They were intent on using it to make a child to sacrifice to the devil, essentially the plot to Roman Polanski's 1968 supernatural classic *Rosemary's Baby*."

Seeing that he was in desperate need, poet and song writer Cherry Vanilla hooked Bowie up with Walli Elmlark who Spitz describes as a "Manhattan-based intellectual...who taught classes at the New York School of Occut Arts and sciences then located on Fourteenth Street, just north of Greenwich Village," and which the author of this article was director of from the mid 1960s for more than a decade, promoting lectures and classes by the who's who of paranormal and UFO experts of that era, including Cleve Backster, Stanley Krippner, Jim Moseley, John Keel - and, of course, Walli Elmlark the White Witch of New York.

As added confirmation of the madness, David was trying to cope with, ex wife Angie Bowie reveals even more details of his fascination and dabbling into the occult in her own personal remembrance, *Backstage Passes: Life on the Wild Side With David Bowie.*

David Bowie

"There was a beautiful Art Deco house on six acres, an exquisite site property and a terrific value at just $300,000, but he took one look at a detail I hadn't noticed, a hexagram painted on the floor of a circular room by the previous owner, Gypsy Rose Lee.

"A great deal of codling and reassurance got us through that crisis, and I went and found the Doheny Drive house. Built in the late fifties or early sixties, it was a white cube surrounding an indoor swimming pool. David like the place, but I thought it was too small to meet our needs for very long, and I wasn't crazy about the pool. In my experience, indoor pools are always a problem.

"This one was no exception, albeit not in any of the usual ways. Its drawback was one I hadn't encountered before and haven't seen or heard of since: Satan lived in it. With his own eyes, David said, he'd seen HIM rising up out of the water one night."

Feeling demonic forces moving in, David felt strongly that he needed an exorcism and asked that his new found friend white witch Walli Elmlark be called upon to lend her assistance to remove the evil from his surroundings.

"A Greek Orthodox Church, in LA would have done it for us (there was a priest available for such a service, the people had told me) but David wouldn't have it. No strangers allowed, he said. So there we stood, with just Walli's instructions and a few hundred dollars' worth of books, talismans, and assorted items from Hollywood's comprehensive selection of fine occult emporia.

"There he (David Bowie) was, then, primed and ready. The proper books and doodads were arranged on a big old-fashioned lectern. The incantation began, and although I had no idea what was being said or what language it was being said in, I couldn't stop a weird cold feeling rising up in me as David droned on and on.

"There's no easy or elegant way to say this, so I'll just say it straight. At a certain point in the ritual, the pool began to bubble. It bubbled vigorously (perhaps "thrashed" is a better term) in a manner inconsistent with any explanation involving air filters or the like."

The rock and roll couple watched in amazement. Angie says she tried to be flippant - "'Well, dear, aren't you clever? It seems to be working. Something's making a move, don't you think?' - but I couldn't keep it up. It was very, very strange; even after my recent experiences I was having trouble accepting what my eyes were seeing."

Angie insists that she would peak through the glass doors which lead to the pool every so often and was dumb founded by what she saw.

"On the bottom of the pool was a large shadow, or stain, which had not been there before the ritual began. It was in the shape of a beast of the underworld; it reminded me of those twisted, tormented gargoyles screaming silently from the spires of medieval cathedrals. It was ugly, shocking, and malevolent; it frightened me.

"I backed away from it feeling very strange, went through the doorway, and told David what I'd seen, trying to be nonchalant but not doing very well. He turned white but eventually became revived enough to spend the rest of the night doing coke. He wouldn't go near the pool, though.

"I still don't know what to think about that night. It runs directly counter to my pragmatism and my everyday faith in the integrity of the "normal" world, and it confuses me greatly. What troubles me the most is that if you were to call that stain the mark of Satan, I don't see how I could argue with you."

"David, of course, insisted that we move from the house as quickly as possible, and we did that, but I've heard from reliable sources (Michael Lipman for one, the property's real estate agent) that subsequent tenants haven't been able to remove the shadow. Even though the pool has been painted over a number of times, the shadow has always come back."

Several years went by and Walli met an untimely passing as she could not remove the demons in her own life, even though she had a dramatic impact on almost everyone she came in contact with. Besides teaching at the School Of Occult Arts And Sciences, Walli teamed up with the likes of T Rex's Marc Bolan (whom she nicked named the Wizzard) and King Crimson's guitarist Robert Fripp. The trio went off to merry old England to record a spoken word album Though The Cosmic Children has never been released the soundtrack was years ahead of its time, centering around those special souls who Walli believed had reincarnated on earth from "elsewhere" at a very important time in the human evolutionary process to pass on the light to others who were destined to change the world through music, literature and an emerging New Age philosophy. The recording is out there somewhere - perhaps safely in the vault of Robert Fripp - who hopefully if he reads this will contact me and allow us to do a limited pressing for those who would truly find this effort transformational.

Walli and I worked mutually for a number of years on several projects and even co-authored a book together. Out of print for decades, once in a while I have seen a copy of Rock Raps Of The Seventies offered on eBay or elsewhere at an exorbitant price.

Somehow I can't exclude the fact that Walli looks down from time to time and perhaps sings along with David Bowie as he performs all over the world in concert. Long recovered from drugs and the dark aspects of occultism, he is now raising a family and going on with his chosen task. And perhaps before you know it his Starman song may take on a reality all it's own if the predicted disclosure about UFOs and extraterrestrials ever comes about in our lifetime.

Hey, I don't deserve a medal. I'm just doing what any good Samaritan UFOlogist would do. . .saving the life of an alien who crashed to Earth. OK truth is my friend Charla took this shot of me on the main street in Sedona in front of a crashed spaceship prop used to attract visitors.

THE AUTHENTIC BOOK OF ULTRA-TERRESTRIAL CONTACTS

ANYONE READING THIS VOLUME WHO WOULD LIKE ADDITIONAL
INFORMATION ON CONTACTING BENEFICIAL ULTRA-TERRESTRIAL
IS ELIGIBLE FOR A FREE 60-MINUTE AUDIO CD NARRATED BY THE
BEST SELLING AUTHOR AND RESEARCHER, BRAD STEIGER.

Simply specify that you want the UFO COMMUNICATIONS CD
and contact the publisher at:

mrufo8@hotmail.com

Tim Beckley, Publisher
Box 753,
New Brunswick, NJ 08903

A free weekly newsletter is also available to all at. . .

WWW.CONSPIRACYJOURNAL.COM

Made in the USA
Middletown, DE
13 September 2021